THOMAS CHATTERTON

CHATTERTON

(From the painting by Henry Wallis, R.W.S., in the National Gallery of British Art.)

THOMAS CHATTERTON

THE MARVELOUS BOY

THE STORY OF
A STRANGE LIFE
1 7 5 2 - 1 7 7 0

BY

CHARLES EDWARD RUSSELL

ILLUSTRATED

University Press of the Pacific
Honolulu, Hawaii

Thomas Chatterton: The Marvelous Boy:
The Story of A Strange Life, 1752-1770

by
Charles Edward Russell

ISBN: 1-4102-1400-1

Copyright © 2004 by University Press of the Pacific

Reprinted from the 1908 edition

University Press of the Pacific
Honolulu, Hawaii
http://www.universitypressofthepacific.com

THOMAS CHATTERTON

With Shakespeare's manhood at a boy's wild heart, —
   Through Hamlet's doubt to Shakespeare near allied
   And kin to Milton through his Satan's pride, —
At Death's sole door he stooped, and craved a dart;
And to the dear new bower of England's art, —
   Even to that shrine Time else had deified,
   The unuttered heart that soared against his side,
Drove the fell point, and smote life's seals apart.

Thy nested home-loves, noble Chatterton,
   The angel-trodden stair thy soul could trace
   Up Redcliffe's spire; and in the world's armed space
Thy gallant sword-play: — these to many an one
Are sweet forever; as thy grave unknown
   And love-dream of thine unrecorded face.

— DANTE GABRIEL ROSSETTI, "Five English Poet

CONTENTS

APPENDIX I

APPENDIX II

APPENDIX III

APPENDIX IV

LIST OF ILLUSTRATIONS

CHRONOLOGY OF THOMAS CHATTERTON

Born at Bristol	November 20, 1752
Admitted to Colston's Charity School	August, 1760
Wrote his first extant poem when ten years old	December, 1762
Published it ("On the Last Epiphany")	January 8, 1763
Published "The Church-Warden and the Apparition"	January 7, 1764
Left Colston's, apprenticed to Lawyer Lambert	July 1, 1767
Published the account of the opening of the Old Bridge	September, 1768
Completed "Aella, a Tragycal Enterlude" before	December, 1768
Correspondence with Horace Walpole	March to July, 1769
Completed his satirical poem "Kew Gardens" about	March, 1769
Had his Indenture cancelled	April 16, 1770
Started for London	April 23, 1770
His friend, Lord Mayor Beckford, died	June 19, 1770
Completed his "Balade of Charitie"	July, 1770
Killed himself in Brooke Street, London	August 24, 1770

AMONG HIS CONTEMPORARIES WERE:

Dr. Samuel Johnson 1709–1784
James Boswell 1740–1795
Edward Young 1681–1765

Thomas Gray 1716–1771
William Collins......................1720–1756
Mark Akenside 1721–1770
Oliver Goldsmith 1728–1774
Bishop Percy........................1728–1811
William Cowper 1731–1800
Charles Churchill 1731–1764
George Crabbe 1754–1832
William Shenstone 1714–1763
William Mason 1724–1797
"Ossian" Macpherson 1738–1796
Hannah More 1745–1833
Joseph Warton 1722–1800
David Garrick 1717–1779
Richard Brinsley Sheridan 1751–1816
Sir Joshua Reynolds 1723–1792
Thomas Gainsborough 1727–1788
The Elder Pitt 1708–1778
Horace Walpole 1717–1797
Lawrence Sterne....................1713–1768
Tobias George Smollett 1721–1771
Samuel Richardson 1689–1761
William Blackstone 1723–1780
William Herschel 1738–1822

PREFATORY NOTE

I HAVE tried in these pages to set forth the plain records of this extraordinary story with hope to do something, however little, however poor and inadequate, to clear from calumny and undeserved reproach the memory of one of the greatest minds and sweetest souls that ever dwelt upon this earth.

That in the short span of his unhappy life this boy should have produced works of the first order of genius, works ever since the marvel of all persons that have considered them, works profoundly affecting the body and the development of English poetry, is the most amazing fact in literature. Next to it in wonder I place the fact that this great spirit, this artist and poet, this lover and benefactor of his kind, this assailant of absolutism, this boy hero of revolt, this leader at seventeen in the army of man, has been kept by false report and malignant slander from his true place in the affections of the race he labored for. And next to this I place the fact, herein, I think, for the first time made clear, that all of these false reports and all of these slanders had no other origin than the petty malice of a spiteful

and vindictive old man. For I deem it impossible
to come from any impartial and first-hand investigation of these matters without the conviction that
Thomas Chatterton would never have been called
a Literary Forger, would never have been a moral
warning to the young nor an outcast among the men
of letters, if he had not offended Horace Walpole,
Earl of Orford.

With what monstrous injustice he has been
branded with that word Forger, how unreasonably
he has been assailed, how far his actual life, full of
love, tenderness, and good deeds, was above the
libels that have been cast upon it, I have labored
here to make plain. For the first time the statements derogatory to Chatterton's character have
been traced from hand to hand back to the one
fountain head, identical in each instance; and for
the first time an attempt has been made to compare
the accepted narrative with the available records.
It may ease others as I was eased to know that the
wonderful boy, whose days were so unutterably sad
and lonely and whose heart was so infallibly kind,
was not a libertine, was not dissolute, was not venal,
and was not a Literary Forger. And it may instruct
others as I was profoundly instructed to know that
in the remarkable vitality of these monstrous false-
hoods he has paid the penalty for attacking privilege
and championing the cause of mankind. For in more

ways than one this boy has been a martyr of democracy, and no one may doubt that if he had fought for absolutism as fiercely as he attacked it, there would now be no need to defend his reputation.

It is time to have done with the prejudice and bigotry that have obscured this glorious name. The world crushed out the life of Thomas Chatterton when he was still a boy. That ought to be enough. With cudgel and savage injustice and cruelty and privation it embittered almost every moment of his existence. That ought to be enough. For more than one hundred years it has dwelt with moral edification upon his poor little errors. That ought to be enough. Possibly now is more profit to be had from considering his magnificent art, the products of his unequaled genius and the natural goodness of his heart. To try in some way to further such consideration was the object of this book.

Some obstacle to a wide reading of Chatterton has been found in the strange and antique garb of the Rowley poems. An attempt is made here to show how slight is this obstacle by printing examples of the poems in their original and others in a modernized form. There will also be found analyses of musical themes employed by Chatterton that may seem to exhibit more clearly the unusual nature of his endowment and the essential beauty of his work.

The materials here used have been drawn chiefly

from the invaluable collection of books, documents, and letters referring to Chatterton, now preserved in the Bristol Museum and Library. The discovery that Barrett knew of and aided the attempted imposture upon Walpole Mr. Edward Bell had briefly noted among the documents in the British Museum, and further investigation, following this vital fact, seemed to show the whole of Barrett's conduct in a light that leaves small room to blame the boy and much to doubt the man. Of the extant biographies I have found that of Professor Wilson and the short life written by Mr. Bell (and used as a preface to Skeat's edition of Chatterton's poems), to be the most accurate as they are also the most interesting and sympathetic. The other lives, being made up chiefly from the errors of Dix and Chalmers, are not available for the purposes of the modern biographer. I have been at pains to verify, so far as possible, from the original sources, all the statements made here concerning Chatterton's career; and whether the result be ill or good, at least this is true, that nothing has been taken for granted nor accepted on light evidence.

I should be much to blame if I omitted from this note an expression of my gratitude to the good city of Bristol that, with a universal and genuine kindness, so long and so often harbored me and furthered in every way my design.   Surely the stranger's path could not have been made pleasanter for him. To many of the citizens of Bristol and many persons elsewhere I am under enduring obligations: to Mr. Alderman Barker, J. P., of Bristol, for his active assistance in securing from the municipal government permission to examine and photograph the Chatterton relics that are now part of the city's treasures; to Mr. L. Acklan Taylor, of the Bristol Library, for unwearied efforts in my behalf; to Mr. Jackson, headmaster of the St. Elizabeth's Hospital school, to the vicar of St. Mary Redcliffe, to Mr. Mayhew, of the British Museum, for generous assistance; to the authorities of the British Museum for permission to examine and photograph the Chatterton relics there, and lastly to the Bodleian Library at Oxford.

Fourteen years have passed since this inquiry began.   If now it bear fruit in a word or a suggestion that may help any one to a better acquaintance with a mind in whose companionship I have found great and always increasing pleasure, I shall be glad.

                                        C. E. R.

New York, November 1, 1907.

THOMAS CHATTERTON

I

AN EARLY DAY SCHOLAR IN POLITICS

THE time was the time of the Roses, Red and White; the England was the England of Henry VI and Edward IV, torn with long dissensions, and at last with civil war. In all such eras are a few minds that the prevailing atmosphere of unrest seems to make nimble to nobler exercises than the trade of blows. One such mind that then illumined and enlivened the ancient busy seaport of Bristol was destined after centuries (so strangely come about the threads of life), profoundly to affect men, manners, and arts whereof its own day had no dream.

Bristol has ever had pride in her commerce and in her churches, both remarkable, and to both this man notably contributed. He was a great merchant, a tower of commercial strength, the legitimate forerunner of modern mercantile princes and potentates, by name William Canynge. His ships sailed all seas known of his age; they brought home rare products from strange far-away regions, like Spain and Portugal, and even, by connection with Genoa and Venice, from the mystical East. He was of a family of merchants. His grandfather, whose name and virtues he repeated, had founded the house and carried it to fame and success, and thrice had been mayor of Bristol; his father, though less distinguished, had managed to steer the family fortunes through the seas of troublous times, and now the younger William far outdid their achievements. He built ship after ship, he grew in wealth and power, he was five times chosen mayor, his fame as the richest and most enterprising merchant in the west spread far abroad, he was known at court and, for all the royal temptation (in those days of rapine) to plunder a man of such reputed wealth, he long escaped unfavorable attention.

He was likewise of an intellectual habit and of taste in the arts; he knew and loved good architecture, he loved learning and had for his times an unusual share of it. His ships might go armed and his captains might pursue methods that in later and more orderly times would insure their hanging; for himself, his ways were ways of pleasantness. Without the city, in a fine terraced garden by a branch of the Avon, he built a house, spacious for those days, a part of which still standing attests eloquently the excellent art of its builder. This Red Lodge had a great hall wherein was a magnificent broad staircase, elegantly carved and adorned, a balcony, justly planned, and a generous fireplace. The beam ends were cut after a chaste design, the ceiling was imposing; all the house, so far as the remains testify, spoke of sound and discriminating judgment and an indomitable sense of esthetic propriety.

He was, in truth, an extraordinary person, this Canynge. The chief line of trade of his paternal house was the woolen staple. William so extended and furthered it that he became in it an international figure, and treaties were made about him and his doings. He had a natural inclining towards politics, not less than towards learning. Almost with manhood he began to take active part in public affairs. First he was chosen bailiff, then sheriff, then mayor, and finally his admiring townsmen sent him to Parliament. His practise was ever towards a prominent part in whatever chanced to be the current event; in Parliament he had a hand in the attainder of Jack Cade, after that fustian rebel's career had made an end; and when it dawned upon the intellect of his day that if the common people had revolted they must have had something to revolt about, he helped to investigate that surpassing strange mystery. The investigation led him upon delicate ground. He was a zealous advocate and personal friend of King Henry VI, and much of the blame for the popular discontent was found (or imagined) to rest upon King Henry's strenuous consort, Queen Margaret; a situation that might have puzzled any statesman. But the Canynge mind was ever in emergency resourceful. The merchant found a way to do his duty by the nation without straining his friendship for the King, who testified to his appreciation of so intelligent a subject by securing special concessions from Denmark for the Canynge woolen trade.

Parliament dissolved, Canynge returned to Bristol and was promptly re-elected mayor. He must have been a most generous soul as well as a canny and a popular. Perdurable tradition has connected his name with more benevolent enterprises than any one man of his times could possibly have sustained, a certain if somewhat awkward testimony to the esteem of his compatriots; but one of his undoubted gifts to Bristol proved to be, in a way, her most valuable possession. A little to the south of his surburban residence rose a hill and thereon (of ancient foundation) a church of St. Mary. Tradition assigned the origin of this church chiefly to the liberality of one Simon de Burton or Bortonne, a famous citizen and six times mayor of Bristol, in the thirteenth century, though tradition was probably wrong. In the time of the elder William Canynge the church had fallen into much decay. The grandfather had begun to rebuild it; the grandson took up the pious work and completed it at his own expense and that not small, for it is a majestic edifice. What share he had in the design of the restoration is lost with more important matters in the dust of the ages; but he had a fancy for building, a clear eye, the sense of beauty, and if the plan had no origin in his mind, doubtless it was of his choosing. The result was the most beautiful specimen of Perpendicular architecture in England and probably the most beautiful in the world. Queen Elizabeth, when she saw St. Mary Redcliffe, declared it to be the fairest and goodliest parish church in her realm, and whatever may have been her shortcomings otherwise, about such things she had a nice and discerning taste. The church is, indeed, a kind of poem in stone, so exquisitely is it proportioned and so faultlessly done. Height, length, breadth, convey an inevitable impression of massive and adorned nobility; between the length of the nave and the height of the tower, between outline and ornamentation, between detail and detail, is such wedded harmony as seems to strike audible notes of pleasure. The main portal has a noble arch, the finials are most graceful, the tracery of eaves and cornice is like lace-work. About it all, merely to look at it, is a singular and romantic charm. The other churches of Bristol, as elsewhere in England, are interesting enough but rather plain; this among parish churches stands almost alone in the rich and intricate beauty of its conception and the perfect adaptation of all its adornments to the general effect. Gazed at from a little distance it seems to be more of the air than of earth and to possess spiritual significance both restful and inspiring.

The crown of all its beauties is the wonderful North Porch, a hexagonal tower of no great height, but sweetly planned and harmoniously decorated, as near perfection as English architecture can show, whereof the clean richness infallibly arrests every observing eye. In this tower, on the east side of the entrance (which has a groined ceiling), was made a spiral staircase, and this led by many steps to a room at the top, lighted by windows in each of the six sides. Here in great locked chests were kept the records of the church and its treasures, the silver urns and vessels of its altar, the moneys that came to it, and in the end, the parchment property deeds of the land in the parish. This place was called the Muniment Room.

Here comes in the other man of this story, the supposed priest, the mysterious person whose very name was afterward for almost a century a thing to precipitate furious controversy, whose very existence is bound in such clouds of endless and baffling speculation that no man may now come to the truth. So meager are the certain facts, so vast and imposing the fabric of romance reared upon them, there is scarcely another character in English history more alluring to futile fancy building. Assuredly there was a

The Famous North Porch of St. Mary Redcliffe.
(The Muniment Room, which contained " Canynge's Coffer " and the old parchments, is at the top, lighted by the narrow windows.)

Thomas Rowley; he seems to have been of the church, he was in Bristol at the time St. Mary Redcliffe was rebuilt. The records of the adjacent see of Wells speak of his ordaining to be an acolyth there. Tradition or wild imagination has assigned him conspicuous share in William Canynge's great work. Whether he was the rich man's dearest friend, confidant and adviser, whether he was a scholar notable in his times, whether he was any friend of learning, or whether, as there is some reason to think, he was no more than a plain and common-place good citizen, nothing certain can be said; and yet, in the strangest way, the mere name of him, the mere suggestion of his shadowy being, has come to be of far more importance in the world than the blazoned deeds of many a less dubious hero.

To the church he had so handsomely recreated the merchant was open handed. Tradition has hung upon the garment of his life a deal of philanthropic embroidery, but of his repeated benefactions to St. Mary Redcliffe is genuine record. In small things and in great there is evidence of his essential goodness; indeed, he must have been a pleasant man to know, a kind of human oasis in the acrid desert of his times, for he had democratic tendencies and a kindly heart. For instance, when his cook died he buried him in the floor of the church at the south

end of the transept, and adorned the tombstone with
emblems of the dead man's craft.   This might mean
merely that William Coke was a master of his art
and testify as much of the mayor's appreciation of
venison pasty as of his democracy, were it not that
Canynge was a passing spare man of ascetic habits,
and that when John Brewer and James Purse-
bearer, also of his household, went likewise the way
of flesh, he honored each with a similar tribute.
Of the general impress he made upon the common
mind of his day there is ample evidence.   It must
have been a sincere affection in which he was held,
for it long survived him and had a curiously indelible
stamp.

He was excellently married, but his children all
died in infancy.   For his wife, Johanna, he cherished
an esteem and a reverent affection rather out of the
common.   When she died he paid to her virtues the
honor of a beautiful effigy in St. Mary Redcliffe,
and a tribute of celibacy that, according to tradition, resulted, strangely enough, in the fall of all
his earthly hopes and the ruin of his public career.

Politically, the times grew worse, the sun of York
began to eclipse the gentle Lancaster, brawl and
riot swelled to open war.   From sincere sympathy
Canynge was a Lancastrian.   In some wonderful
way he so held his course that abating no jot of his
affection for Henry he kept his state and fortune

after the White Rose had triumphed and Edward IV was come to the throne. But he went not altogether unpunished. After a time the genial monarch came down to Bristol on what may be termed a visit of inspection for his own profit, and made himself a guest at the Red Lodge. Canynge lavishly entertained his powerful and erratic visitor, but was doubtless not grieved when he departed. The whole incident might well have been viewed with concern, for it appears that Edward, having utilized his opportunity as a guest to learn much of the wealth of Bristol (where there had been many Lancastrians), soon after levied upon the city a fine "for his peace." That is to say, he replenished his exchequer at the expense both of his late foes and his more recent entertainers. From Canynge he took three thousand marks in ten vessels, a predation that must have been a heavy blow to the merchant.

Royal Edward had other attentions in store. There was at court in those days a titled lady of the Widville family that for reasons of his own the amiable king desired to have married, and it may have struck the kingly mind that Canynge, being a commoner, would feel flattered by an offer of such a union. Obviously the merchant had other views of the matter. We have no knowledge of the fair lady Widville, appointed to confer upon him the honor of her hand, but we have some knowledge of Edward IV, and we may suppose that more reasons than fidelity to the memory of his late wife had weight with the merchant. He demurred to the royal will and was unmoved when the masterful Edward insisted. It was an age when the ax was handy and the headsman industrious; Canynge had known in his own city some horrid instances of what kings could do with these instruments of their pleasure, and he lost no time in assuring his safety. With what part of his means was tractile he fled to the church, took holy orders, and sanctuary shut its doors in the baffled king's face.

Esoteric consolations seem to have availed much with the undismayed Canynge. He retired presently to the Abbey at Westbury. The rest of his life, eight years, he spent in the ministrations of his office and in good deeds, among which was the founding of a college. He died November 7, 1474, Dean of Westbury. Two effigies of him adorn St. Mary Redcliffe. One showing him in his magisterial robes as mayor of Bristol was made in his lifetime and designed to lie by the side of his wife's image. The other, copied from this, is carved in alabaster and shows him garbed as the Dean of Westbury. The rare tribute of two effigies in one church is sufficent evidence of the esteem in which the community held this unusual man. If the sculptured face, as is probable, resembled the living, the merchant prince was of a thoughtful and somewhat melancholy expression and must have been an interesting figure.

Something of his story is told in this epitaph in the wall above the alabaster figure:

> M[r] William Caning[s], ye Richest marchant of y[e] towne
> of Bristow afterwards chosen 5 time[s] mayor of y[e] said
> towne for y[e] good of y[e] comon wealth of y[e] fame.   Hee
> was in order of Priesthood 7 years & afterwar[ds]
> Deane of Westbury and died y[e] 7th of Novem 1474
> which said William did build within y[e] said towne of
> Westbury a Colledge (which his canons) & y[e] said
> William did maintaine by space of 8 years 800 handy
> crafts men, besides carpenters & masons, every day
> 100 men.   Besides King Edward y[e] 4th had of y[e] said
> William 3000 marks for his peac[e] to be had in 2470[1]
> tonnes of shiping.
> These are ye names·of his shiping with their bur[then]

TONNES		TONNES	
ye Mary Canings	400	ye Mary Batt	220
ye Mary Redcliffe	500	Ye Little Nicholas	140
ye Mary & John	900	ye Margarett	200
ye Galliott	050	ye Katharine of Boston	22
ye Katherine	140	A ship in Ireland	100

Close at hand is this metrical tribute, no doubt of a later date:

---

[1] Thus the inscription.   The tonnage of the ships in the list is not "2470" but 2672.   But these carvers of epitaphs were a careless race.

No age nor time can wear out well won fame
the stones themselves a featly worke doth shew
from senceless grave we ground may men's good name
And noble minds by ventrous deeds we know
A lanterne cleere settes forth a candell light
A worthy act declares a worthy wight
the Buildings rare that here you may behol^d
to shrine his Bones deserves a tomb^e of gold
the famous Fabricke that he here hath don^{ne}
shines in the sphere as glorious as the son^{ne}
What needs more words ye future world he sou^{ght}
An set ye pompe & pride of this at nought
heaven was his aime let heaven be still his stat^{ion}
that leaves such work^s for others imitation.

Of Rowley there is no more record.   He came and
went like a shadow across the face of events, with
only to tell of his passing a scantly discernible name.

II

Dreams and Realities

WILLIAM, thus the last of the Canynges, had been dust three hundred years; part of his beautiful house had been demolished and the rest obscured; the name of Thomas Rowley had faded from the human memory; the life records of historic merchant and legendary friend with all their ways and works were knee-deep in the dead leaves of oblivion; when suddenly both were revived to fame through the appearance of a figure much more remarkable than either.

Almost in the shadow of St. Mary Redcliffe, in a narrow and now squalid street that bounds the churchyard on the north, is a little two-storied stone schoolhouse, fronted by a thin strip of verdure and abutting rearward upon the remains of an ancient garden. It is almost two hundred years old, the seat of a school founded by a charitable tradesman of Bristol in 1733. Within, the square uncompromising schoolroom occupies the front part of the ground floor; the rest of the house is the narrow quarters of the master and his family. Over this Pyle Street school, from 1738 to 1752, presided one

Thomas Chatterton, much given to conviviality and a little to music; on Sundays a singing man, or subchanter, in the Bristol Cathedral; on other days chiefly busied (outside of his school) at a club the main object of which seems to have been to promote among its members a habit of excessive drinking. An ordinary man of ordinary stock, he was the first of his tribe in a long line of succession to depart from one calling. Father and son, the Chattertons had been sextons of St. Mary Redcliffe for one hundred and fifty years. In his case, the innovation was hardly of his own choosing. His father, John Chatterton, had survived in active discharge of the sexton's duties beyond the time when the son must seek a livelihood. He was thirty-five when the post became vacant, and being then set in other ways and uninclined toward the cold *hic jacets* of the dead, the place of his fathers passed to the possession of his sister's husband, Richard Phillips.

The schoolmaster was of no scholarly habit; his mind was not thoughtful, nor, indeed, above mediocrity, and yet he was not destitute of taste and some crude fancy for literature. He knew something about music and even composed a catch for three voices, a kind of drinking song, said to be an extremely dull performance. He sang well, he loved good roaring company at the ale house, he was careless, plodding, unaspiring, and without a trait to distinguish him from his roistering kind. In fact, a colorless person, even in his bibulous way of life not beyond the general custom of his age; for he was not quite a sot. He had to wife Sarah Young, a decent, plain woman, a farmer's daughter, and able to read and write, whom he had married in a near-by hamlet, to wit, Chipping-Sudbury, where she lived. She was less than half his age at the time, that is, she was sixteen and he thirty-five. He seemed to care little for her, and some observant cronies, seeing that he preferred the tavern to home and roisterers to his wife's company, wondered that he had wed at all. "To get a house-keeper," was his curt explanation of this mystery. They had one child, a little girl, Mary, not different from other children. A son, Giles Malpas Chatterton, named in honor of the builder of the Pyle Street schoolhouse, had died in infancy. The schoolmaster was not of robust constitution, his habits made against health, and he died August 7, 1752, aged thirty-nine, of a cold and fever, due to exposure, probably when he was drunk.

Three months after his death, that is to say, on November 20, 1752, in the rear room up-stairs in the little schoolhouse, where the windows look out upon the remnants of the garden, his third child, a son, came into this world, and was christened with his name.

The father had been shiftless and improvident; he left nothing but a scant handful of books and a memory none too fragrant, and the young widow was in straits for bread. There were four to care for; besides the children her mother was dependent upon her. A new master was appointed for the Pyle Street school, and the dwelling was his. As soon as might be the little family moved, going into a poor house up a dark court on Redcliffe hill, almost opposite the main portal of the church. Here Mrs. Chatterton settled into a grim struggle against starvation, making her way by keeping a little day school for very young girls (a kind of forerunning kindergarten), and by toiling industriously with her needle. She was a large, motherly soul, simple, unimaginative and affectionate. The little girls that at her knee learned their alphabets and reading became so fond of her that always afterward they looked upon her as on a foster mother, and when they grew up and were matrons they went back to visit and assist her in her age and heavy troubles.

When the boy Thomas was five years old his mother sent him to the same Pyle Street school, in the house where he had been born. After a time the master returned him home with the information that he was too hopelessly dull to learn his letters. At home they thought him rather taciturn and strange than dull. He was a grave little man and a lonely, but handsome and of an expression intelligent though melancholy; slender and fair, with long light brown hair. His disposition puzzled his mother and might have puzzled those of more wit. He was at once exceedingly sensitive and exceedingly proud, affectionate and moody, and the oddest thing was that he had little interest in childish amusements, did not care much to play with other children, sometimes wept for no apparent reason and was fond of solitude and most fond of St. Mary Redcliffe.

All the threads of this story lead to St. Mary Redcliffe. Thomas Chatterton had been born in its shadow, he dwelt across the street from it, his ancestors for generations back had been employed in it, and now, his relative Richard Phillips, its sexton (sometimes called his uncle), was the only person outside of his own household in whom he manifested an affectionate interest. With Phillips he struck up a close friendship; they were much together, a strange and ill-assorted couple, for the sexton was elderly and the boy small for his age. Day after day they walked through the church or in the churchyard, the boy clinging to the old man's hand and hearing with insatiable appetite all the centuries' accumulated lore about the place with which he was strangely fascinated. It was the home of legends, time out of mind the sexton's inheritance, and it is the ancient privilege of legend handed down from generation to generation to lose nothing on its way. Probably many of the stories of the church that passed from the gray-headed sexton to his little charge would have added a new and picturesque quality to plain history.

The boy that was too dull to be taught his letters presently learned them without teaching, lying prone upon the floor of his mother's house with the cover of an old music book or a great black-letter Bible opened before him and tracing out the big blocks with his little fingers. His mother and his sister helping him, he quickly learned to read, and developed almost at once a passion for reading that fell not far short of a mania. He read everything in his mother's house and, hungering always for more, began to forage in the houses of the few neighbors that had books.

In those days there was no fiction for children and precious little for adults. People satisfied the imaginative longings by constructing what romance they could from the bony material of their own lives and environments, often hard enough, or went without. The boy could find little reading that did not partake of the juiceless life of the age, but upon all he fell as one starving; some scraps of history, Spenser's Faerie Queene, the poems of Gray and of Pope, scientific treatises, the few and poor magazines of the day, whatever he could find. These were his playmates,

comrades, confidants, and friends — books and the
church, the beautiful church that from the first
seemed to dominate all his thoughts and dreams.
For hours together he would lie and gaze and brood
upon it, stretched under a tree in the meadows that
once lay to the southward and are now long obliterated by squares of ugly brick. Daily he roamed
about it, sometimes with his friend the old sexton,
sometimes alone, taking into his childish mind history and legends of building and builders, and with
infinite delight learning and repeating even the small-
est details. There was endless store of material,
the effigies, the moldering arms of William Penn's
father, that doughty old warrior, the quaint inscriptions, the painted glass, the air of romance and
mysticism. Stories were thick about him. There
was the great whale bone about which the romancers
had rewoven the old ballad tale of the Great Dun Cow
and Guy of Warwick, the tale of Dunsmore and its
weird creature. No child could see such a thing
without asking what it meant, that huge yellow bone;
no imaginative child could hear the story, that this
was the very rib of the identical Great Cow slain in
combat by the adventurous knight, without a stirring
to long trains of fantastic dreamings. Who was Guy
of Warwick and what other deeds of prowess did
he ? And there was the crumbling image of the old
Crusader, in all his arms, suggestive of chivalry and

the Lion Heart. There was the alabaster effigy of Canynge, so unusual and beautiful, and there was that baffling, half-told, strange story of the epitaph. What boy could read that and not burn with curiosity to know what it meant? "For his peace" — why for his peace? And all that confiscated shipping the very names of which seemed to suggest queer old quays loaded with strange bales from the east, and queerly dressed sailors, pirates and perils, and the mystery of the seas when there was no America. And this Canynge — five times Mayor of Bristol, the richest man of his age, the munificent builder of the church that engrossed the boy's thoughts — what manner of man had he been? There was his image, the fine, clear-cut face, the lofty forehead, the haunting suggestion of pain and melancholy, and of high, resolute will; and then again in the glory of the magisterial robes. So men were dressed like that in Canynge's time; richly and beautifully dressed like that! What a sight it must have been when such men walked in a procession! He had seen on Palm Sunday in the church that he loved and dreamed over and brooded upon the peculiar ceremony of Rush-bearing, the mayor of his own day walking at the head of the stately show, the civic dignitaries, the choir boys. What must it have been when men wore gorgeous robes like Canynge's, or went about the street clad in armor and bearing swords and pikes?

As he grew older and wandered farther in his lonely childish way, dreaming and musing, those streets seemed the perfect background of his fancies, the quaint, narrow old thoroughfares, lined with brown cross-timbered houses, whereof the upper stories projected successively farther over the sidewalks. The very names were suggestive, Corn Street, Wine Street, and the like, being (as in some old continental cities like Lucerne and Leyden) relics of ancient market customs. Part of the old city wall still stood, crossing the city with a great arch whereon was, strangely placed, a little Gothic chapel, with painted windows, a silent tantalizing witness of bygone days; and then going on up the hill with embrasures for archers and slits for cross-bow men, things the sight of which would bear in upon any boy a whole romance. To reach this marvel he must cross a bridge, built up like the old Bridge of London with houses on each side of the way, a strange structure of the fourteenth century, and he knew that over it had trooped the soldiers of York and Lancaster, that its sleepy old arches had resounded with jingle of armor and clash of broadsword, that cross-bow bolts and long arrows had whistled about it. Not far from the bridge but away from the city wall he found the old Temple Church, its tower leaning over as if it were about to fall and yet never falling. Why should it lean over like that? And was this the church built by the Templars, the gallant Crusaders that had been to Palestine and fought with Richard? Was this their visible work, had they gone in procession in and out of that door? Then there was that strange place, St. Peter's Hospital, built in the age of Elizabeth, and St. Stephen's Church, curiously carved and richly ornamented, and St. Ewin's, the church that in the old brave times was Bristol Minster. His father had been a singing-man, his mother had told him, in the present Bristol Cathedral; here was the place that in the older days had been the center of the religious life of the town, the great authorities of the church had gathered there. And then there was that wonderful old Norman gateway close by the Cathedral; what did that mean? It was so large that people lived in it; the gateway to the old Abbey, he had been told. That must have been a great place when the monks thronged in and out and the cloisters still stood.

But in all these wonders there was none like his own St. Mary Redcliffe, most beautiful of all the churches of Bristol, the home and goal of his fancies. The long nave, the arched transept, the silent aisles, the chancel filled with colored twilight, — he peopled these from the churchyard and the tombs until the persons of an imaginary drama became as real to him as anything he saw. Nothing is commoner among children that have the least imagination than these mental operations in which suppositious beings take part in a continuous action stretched over months or years, daily added to and revised until the narrative assumes the importance of verity. And whereas the average child has, in his daily play, a thousand avenues for the venting of his imaginings, feigning this or that with his playmates, feigning at going to school, or keeping house, or marching armies, this boy had but one. For him, a lonely unfriended waif, there was but one. The church was everything to him, playmate, comrade, friend; it took all the place of toys and playground; life for him seemed to begin there and end. There all the actors in his imaginary drama were connected with the church. There he gathered the fragments of the story of William Canynge, the gorgeous rebuilding of this sacred place, the beautiful house, the splendor and pomp of Canynge's state; and long meditations, long associations with the creatures of his brain, made them seem living to him. They would have seemed so, in a measure, to an ordinary boy, but this boy was not ordinary. He had from the beginning an abnormal imagination, beyond precedent, almost beyond belief; and in his solitary, cheerless way of life his natural gift had so grown upon him that the dead heroes he dreamed of walked and talked with him and became sharers of his daily experiences. Sitting alone in the transept hour after hour, the carved

image of Canynge before him, the tombstones of
Master Coke and Master Brewer at his feet, the
story slowly filled and possessed his mind, the romance of the generous merchant prince, the author
and begetter of that beauty he worshiped, the mind
that had seen this wonderful place in his visions,
perhaps, before a stone had been laid or a beam
cut. He saw him in the glory of the Red Lodge,
he saw the fleet of ships and piles of goods, he saw
him building this church, he saw him mayor, at the
head of great processions, the wise director of his
city's affairs in troublous times; he saw him defy a
king and abandon all his possessions rather than
yield to tyrannical authority; and again in the quiet
sanctuary of Westbury, secure amid his studies. And
this great man was so generous and compassionate,
no doubt in those days if there was a youth or even
boy, no matter how poor he might be, that wished to
do great things in the world and become famous, this
man would help him. Being so rich he must have
had plenty of books, and loving books he must have
loved the men that wrote them. No doubt at the
Red Lodge, with knights in armor and all things beautiful about, were scholars and writers, historians and
poets like those of whom he had been reading. Every
normal boy has a hero, flesh and blood, or one he
has heard or read of. To this boy Canynge was
more than hero, for this figure conjured from the

past became the inseparable companion of his dreamy wanderings.

Besides the church and Red Lodge there were other reminders of Canynge; at home one of the most familiar of daily sights was suggestively coupled with that name. Those chests in the Muniment Room at the top of North Porch, "Mr. Canynge's Coffer," as the sexton called one of them, and the others, contained parish deeds and records, and some years before it had been necessary to consult these documents. The chests were locked, the keys had been lost, and the chests being forced open with an ax were left unsecured when such papers as were needed had been taken out. The parchments with which the chests were filled became accessible, and being regarded as valueless were kicked about the Muniment Room, and got abroad. The boy's father had spied a use in them, and bringing home ample supplies from repeated excursions had made of them excellent covers for his pupils' books. The supply exceeded the demand; some old parchments still lay about the Chatterton house or were used by the prudent housewife for thread papers and so forth, all from Canynge's Coffer, all directly connected with his hero and suggesting the ideal life at Red Lodge. It would have been a dull boy that with such materials could not loose back his imagination to the days when processions of singing monks threaded the dim aisles,

when knights jousted on the meadows close at hand,
when York and Lancaster clashed in the streets of
Bristol, when the now obliterated castle was a prison
for the beaten Lancastrians, when some of them
were put to death at the High Cross, when the city
wall was manned with soldiers, when the Red Lodge
was built in the midst of gardens sloping to the water,
when stone by stone arose the airy fabric of the church,
when Bristol was but a little seaport, its streets
filled with strangely armed men, and its harbors
with vessels of strange shapes, when it was smaller
still, when it was a Saxon settlement commanded
by a castle, when it was an outpost thrust into the
hostile country by the fierce invaders, when it held
the Danes at bay, when the huts of savage woad-
painted Britons huddled about the Avon and on
those banks the Druid priests had cut themselves
with strange knives. Of all these things the boy
had read and read, and here were the scenes where
they had been and where now, to his imagination,
wrapped in his dreams, the old actors returned to
the old places, knights and monks and merchant
prince lived again.

In these years he was a strange boy, loving solitude and his own thoughts, mostly without boy playmates or play, often silent and abstracted, sometimes
speechless for so much as two days together, startling plain people (as were his mother's friends) by

looking fixedly at them evidently without seeing them, absorbed in contemplation, shutting himself into the attic with a book, refusing food, and the like abnormalities. He had a disconcerting way of sitting in company with his eyes fixed on vacancy while the important affairs of the neighborhood, the price of butter and the like pertinent topics, were discussed about him, and then returning suddenly from a far journey to ask what had been talked about. He was sometimes so absent-minded and far gone in his abstraction that he did not hear when he was directly addressed. If he played with other children, which was seldom, he knew but one play and that was that he should be the master, ruler, or commander. From his earliest years other children seemed to yield instinctively to him, that was the odd thing, and never he yielded to another. He was ordinarily most truthful and obedient, but his mother and sister noted that he would fall sometimes into violent fits of weeping for no apparent cause and when pressed to know why he would be at a loss for an answer and say he had been beaten when there was no such matter. He seemed in a way to have had no youth, for he passed from infancy to a state where with mature gravity and knowledge he talked of abstruse subjects and bore himself with a dignity and presence that seem to have moved some observers to wonder and some to amusement. He was not always depressed; sometimes he was a cheerful and most entertaining companion in the home circle, discoursing of the books he had read and explaining to his mother and sisters matters they had dreamed not of. But there was always latent in him a somber and even sorrowful regard that was above and contradicted his mirth. He grew handsomer with the years. His long hair curled and he had wonderful gray eyes that seemed to look clean through one; steady clear eyes, so marvelous that some persons were fascinated by them and thought they could see his soul in their depths. Few that observed them attentively failed to feel strangely attracted to the boy. His pride and his courage were alike extraordinary, and yet he was sensitive and sympathetic, and what was odd in one so self-reliant and so much alone, he was passionately devoted to his mother and sister. A more affectionate nature never lived, and all the wealth of it was poured out upon the little home circle in the poor dingy brick house up a nasty court in Bristol. His mother and his sister Mary were the idols of his heart and first among the dreams of his career was the dream of what he would do for them. For on another side of his nature he was already planning at times about his way in life, and he knew quite well that he was not as other boys were.

He was often absent from home hours together and

when sought for at meal time — for the painful
British regularity was hard upon the good mother —
they found him dreaming about in St. Mary Redcliffe
(usually at the tomb of Canynge), or tucked away
somewhere with a book. He had rather read than
eat, a fact that caused Mrs. Chatterton much concern, as arguing something unwholesome in her off-
spring. When found it was in disgrace that he was
led to the table, for shall it not be criminal to be
late to one's meals? And sometimes much search
was necessary and then punishment followed, the
chastening that was held to be proper for a haughty
spirit in youth.

The wisdom that enables us to prescribe for the
government of other people's children so much
better than for our own was not withheld from Mrs.
Chatterton's women friends. They had observed
Thomas well and with great concern, and the con-
census of their opinion was unfavorable. What he
needed was severity and much of it. Doubtless with
the best intentions they delivered this sage counsel
upon the perplexed mother. There was indeed no
need, as Mercutio says. In that sweet age, wherever
children were the birch hung by the Bible and had
at least equal honor. Parents had mind upon one
scriptural command if no other and spared not.
Whipping was a means of grace for children, and
should a parent neglect his child's salvation? On

one occasion his mother, out of all patience with his unboyish ways, beat him with unusual severity. He endured without a murmur, but when it was over he remarked pathetically, "It is hard to be beaten for reading."

What to do with such a son must have been a sore puzzle to the widow whose wit and income were alike small. For the children of the poor in those days the path was hard and usually led one way. Occasionally one born in poverty achieved by prodigious endeavor some eminence, but the instances were dismally few. Such an exception, conspicuous in Bristol not long before, was still well remembered. Edward Colston, who, beginning obscurely, had made fame and fortune as a merchant, was a liberal benefactor of his native city and some of his philanthropy had naturally followed the suggestion of his own ascent. That is to say, he had founded in 1708 a charity school wherein one hundred poor boys were to be trained for mercantile careers. To make their election sure they were to be provided for in every way, with lodging, clothing, food, as well as tuition. But the number was strictly limited, the pressure for admission very great, and the widow Chatterton must have felt overjoyed and thankful when, a vacancy occurring at Colston's, the intercession of friends and her own endeavors won the place for her boy when he was eight years old.

Colston's School, as it was in Chatterton's Time.

(From an old water-color in the Bristol Museum.)

At that time and for many years afterward there was in England no such institution as we should call a public school, and the generality of poor children got their smattering of knowledge in the private schools founded by the philanthropic, or in schools maintained in some instances by the parishes, or went without, as fate and chance might direct. In other words, the rich fared well enough, the poor shifted for themselves and for most part ill, for it was an ignorant age. Charity schools like Colston's were benevolent in design and oppressive in practise. The prevailing theory seemed to be that the schools were mills and the children therein raw material of an inferior nature sent upon the teachers for their sins, to be ground and hammered and beaten into shape. At Colston's the knowledge deemed essential for a mercantile career was put into the boys' heads by the genial method of brad-awl and hammer. The pupils lived like machines, arose early, toiled assiduously at arithmetic, penmanship, compound interest, book-keeping and the like succulent matters and were released very late. On one day in the week a half-holiday was thoughtfully provided; the rest of the time they were captives to a hideous system of manufacturing shopkeepers' assistants.

And here begins the first of the mysteries we are to deal with. Nothing more repulsive than such a place could have been devised for the boy of dreams. What had he to do with interest tables and the proper form of a bill of lading? In all this he had no conceivable concern, he whose mind was rapt upon Canynge and chivalry, who dwelt perpetually in a land of strange visions. The whole institution filled his soul with loathing. He had no idea of being a shopkeeper or clerk, he cared nothing about weights and measures. What should the knights and ladies of his romance do with the computing of bales of cloth and hogsheads of tobacco? What were to him the dull details and hard rectangles of commercial science? In one day he passed from books and St. Mary Redcliffe and long ways of rhapsody and meditation to the atmosphere of bustling trade. And yet, pitchforked into this dreary treadmill, the amazing thing is that he not only accepted all its hard conditions and acquitted himself manfully and with scrupulous attention to his duties, but he dreamed on as before. His outward activities had undergone a violent change; the soul and the soul's real aims and life remained as before. He was a faithful student at Colston's, he learned his arithmetic, performed his sums, was taught to distinguish between troy weight and avoirdupois, to compute bills and master double-entry; he even managed to obey most of the rules and win the approval of his masters, but he still found time for the things he loved, he still read, dreamed, thought, and incessantly laid by stores of such knowledge as were never taught in a charity school. I do not know how he did it. The soul that would not have been crushed in that place must have been of extraordinary texture. Other boys have kept upon their chosen way in spite of discouragements and disadvantages, — Samuel Johnson, Napoleon, Disraeli, Keats, many others; none of these was shut up in a commercial school at eight years of age and bound in by an iron system through which he must break with invincible determination to find the interests he had taken for his own.

Yet he was no model boy and teacher's pet, he was no cad boy digging tirelessly at the dry roots of school-tasks to be patted upon the head by clergymen and shown to admiring visitors. There was nothing flaccid about Thomas Chatterton. He was a flesh and blood boy, able to laugh as well as to weep, having boy chums in the dormitory, hating some, at least, of his teachers with great heartiness, and seeing quite through the others as keen-witted, normal boys often do; liked among his comrades, positive and successful enough to excite some envy, likely to break over the discipline when he saw fit and able at all times to take care of himself. A manly boy, still much preferring solitude and often afflicted with fits of depression; a boy with two sides to his nature as other boys have had and survived, sometimes exceedingly sad and lonely and sometimes bright and a genial companion, but always self-possessed and sure of himself.

But while with unchanged dreams he held his way at Colston's, two influences he encountered there wholly changed the current of his life. The first of these had relation to his brooding melancholy. While he had good enough friends among the boys, one Baker of whom we shall hear further, and others, he was really intimate with none among them. The one friend in the place that he cared for was Thomas Phillips, who was not a pupil at all but an usher or assistant teacher. This must have been a rather remarkable young man. He studied literature, he wrote verses (whether ill or well the world will never know), he had an enthusiasm for self-culture, and with an unusual generosity he strove to inspire in his young charges the love of these intellectual pleasures; a gratuitous kindness remarkable in a place wholly given up to the Bounderby theory of education. In one of his pupils his ministrations awoke an instantly responsive chord. From the time Thomas Phillips taught Chatterton to make verses the boy's intervals of gloomy depression returned no more. The soul within had lacked the saving grace of expression; it was for expression that unconsciously he had been tearing his heart and beating the bars. With expression he found the secret of something like peace and he turned to verse-making as a tired man comes home. The way along which Phillips started him was at the first a beaten track; it was not long before he had made his own path and that through untried fields.

The usher was a gentle youth and the boy loved and esteemed him, but even with Phillips he had no close confidences. Of the Grand Romance he revealed nothing, he would not tell even this good friend anything about his inner life with Canynge and Rowley and the nights at the Red Lodge. Gradually in his dreamings and wanderings the drama had taken shape and daily lived and moved before him. Somewhere in his interminable studies and searchings he had come upon Thomas Rowley. What he really knew of this mysterious figure, for how much of the eventual creation he found warrant or suggestion, we shall never divine. But in the Grand Romance Rowley became the hero.

It was the oddest hero-making that ever entered a boy's mind. It made Rowley not a knight, a warrior, nor a performer of daring deeds, but a studious and gentle monk of St. John's Church. According to the romance, he and William Canynge had been schoolmates and had then cemented an ideal friendship that lasted through their lives. When Canynge became rich he was able to gratify his taste for learning and the arts, and Rowley was his constant companion in such lofty pursuits. They drew to Red Lodge the best scholars of their region, all the wits, the poets, the writers. Canynge sent Rowley to the monasteries to collect ancient manuscripts, drawings, and choice specimens of the works of early artists. Many of the manuscripts were in the Saxon tongue, and these Rowley, who was a very learned man, translated for his wealthy patron. He was an antiquarian also; he wrote profound treatises on the customs and literature of earlier times. As the boy's mind waxed apace and he himself found the long-sought vent for his creative energies, Rowley became a poet and a dramatist, urged thereto by the benevolent encouragement of his friend. He wrote poems of his own and he gathered and translated the poems of others, and in all he was supported and richly rewarded by Canynge.

There were other persons in the drama. To the feasts of soul at the Red Lodge came John Carpenter, afterward Bishop of Winchester; John Iscamm, another priest; Sir Thybbot Gorges,[1] a nobleman of the neighborhood, and others, and their sessions must have been pleasant affairs, for all these could sound the lyre on occasion and were interested in literature and art. Of these gatherings

[1] Sir Theobold Gorges was a veritable character in Canynge's time and lived at Wraxhall, near Bristol. He is mentioned in a deed of Canynge's to St. Mary Redcliffe Church, and it was in this document that Chatterton must have encountered his name.

Canynge and Rowley were the inspiring forces. Canynge often suggested subjects for Rowley's pen; in return the poet celebrated the goodness and benefactions of his illustrious patron; the relations between them were not the formal relations of priest and parishioner, but of two very dear and congenial friends.

This is an outline of the story as Chatterton created it. To this framework he constantly added details. The consistence of the narrative was re-markable; it stretched over six or seven years of his life, and its developments at different periods all cohered with the outline. No doubt the dream so filled his lonely hours that it ceased to be a dream. All the characters in it and all their deeds and ways and sayings he came to know as well as he knew the deeds and ways of the people about him. He had odd little traits to tell of them, the things one accumu-lates from intimate observation. His real life was spent in their companionship; they were the ever-ready refuge from the world of boy-beaters and gross-minded persons that had no concern above profits. He mused and pondered over it, and into that region withdrew to dwell alone.

Perhaps his reticence with Phillips was because he perceived that his friend was wholly modern and conventional in his tastes; perhaps it was because the other influence I have yet to tell of, as lamentable as

Phillips's was beneficent, grew then upon him. We are far yet from understanding any part of the subtle chemistries by which the environment out of tune and harsh affects some temperaments. Colston's, an excellent school for salesmen, was perdition for a poet. The first plunge into the commercial spring struck a chill of abhorrence to the boy's very soul. He saw at once how little advantage lay there for him. With infinite joy he had hailed the idea of going to school, because he thought he should have unlimited opportunity to learn; but on an early holiday, when he was visiting home and his mother asked him about his prospects, he summed the whole situation in a word. "I could learn more at home," he said quietly, "they have not enough books there to teach me." It was even so and worse than he knew. The daily forced grinding of matter not merely uninteresting but utterly repellent and mentally indigestible was poisonous to him; the daily observation of the principles of business, the daily life in the atmosphere of gain, while it sharpened his wits and opened to him something of the nature of mankind, slowly induced a cynical and coldly humorous habit of mind directly at war with his finer spirit.

As happens sometimes in cases of powerful intellect, two men grew up within him. On one side he was dreamy, affectionate, absorbed in romantic speculation, a citizen of airy cloud-land; on the other side a reasoning observer of his fellow men, disillusioned and skeptical. He learned early to look quite through the deeds of men, to weigh causes and motives, to distrust others and to draw farther within himself. Most ill things have some use. From this acquired cynicism he speedily learned to accept nothing for granted, to despise all conventional dogma and to reject as childish and absurd the surviving relics of feudalism. It is odd that one whose artistic sympathies were wholly medieval should on his active side go so far in advance of his age. If we are to cling to the theory that the normal man must be all of a piece, all progressive or all reactionary, all artist or all politician, we shall never solve this puzzle. The truth is that while he toiled at the tasks of Colston's the dreamer of Rowley slept and the other Chatterton looked about him with cynical disfavor; released from the bench and the chains the dreamer sprang up to life, the galley-oarsman was forgotten.

III

The Rift in the Clouds

The galley-slave labored with exactitude and full, however reluctant, service, and the activities of the other nature were inexhaustible. We have no record of another mind more insatiable of effort. The regimen at Colston's left him little time for any other employment than his studies, and it must be borne in mind that his attention to his mother and sister never slackened. Yet here are some of the things he found time to do: he studied heraldry until he made himself an expert in the intricate science, until probably no man in England knew more of it or had readier or more understanding command of its terms; he wrote much poetry and some prose; he dug deep into the legends as well as the actual history of Bristol; he studied the works of standard English poets and stored his memory with tales, scenes, songs, and lines from them; he read in history, theology, medicine and what science was then available to the average investigator; gathered a good working knowledge of ancient arms and armor, of medieval life and manners, of old English ballads; studied the forms and shapes of early English text; mastered the quaint penmanship of old parchments; learned much about music and something about drawing; read the newspapers; kept in the current of events; formed acquaintances outside the school (all adults); borrowed and read their books and controverted their opinions. I shall not pretend to say how in a school where the sessions began at seven in the morning and lasted until five in the afternoon, and every boy must be in bed at eight o'clock in the evening, these achievements were possible, but there is the record; he did all these things. He had, to be sure, a mind that seemed to hunger and thirst after labor, a mind intolerant of repose; but such a mind highly developed in a grown man could hardly perform these prodigies, and this was a boy passing from his eighth to his sixteenth year.

Colston's occupied a large and rather sightly building at the beginning of what is called St. Augustine's Back, a rise of land from the harbor, a branch of the Avon, to the College Green where the Cathedral stands. The harbor was in front, lengthwise, and in the perspective for many rods; at Colston's end was the old Drawbridge; along the water much shipping. The town came close about, mostly in front and towards the east or on the right of one facing as Colston's faced. In that direction was the fashionable Queen's Square, adorned in the center with a frightful equestrian statue of William III, the one discordant note in the antique harmony of the town, and near this square was the City Library, presently the object of the boy's particular attention, for the dearest quest of his life was books, books, always books. Where there are now thousands of books were not then scores. With extraordinary stupidity access to the few libraries was made as difficult as possible; it was thought well that those that God had ordained to a lowly walk of life should not have too much opportunity to become learned, perhaps lest they should be restless under the divine decree, perhaps with a reasonable fear that they might speedily outstrip their betters. A few persons of means gathered about them small collections of precious volumes and to such persons in Bristol the boy was irresistibly attracted.

One of these was destined to exert upon all the rest of his life a malignant influence. Very close to Colston's on St. Augustine's Back was then dwelling William Barrett, a surgeon of considerable note in Bristol and possessed of some vestiges of taste for literature and antiquities. He was then and had been for years engaged in a task that is one of the monuments of wasted human industry. With inconceivable pains and labor he was writing a huge history of Bristol, a work so full of errors and inaccuracies that it is worthless as anything but a curiosity. He was a cold, calculating person, of somewhat

slender intellect and much centered in himself and
his great project, but the owner of a small library.
The boy seemed to scent books as bees scent honey;
in some way he managed to make the surgeon's
acquaintance and eventually to extract books from
him.   After a time, for reasons of his own, Barrett
chose to encourage the boy's visits and the two
became frequent companions.

The chief recourse of those that had no books of
their own nor admission to the few collections mis-
called "public" was then to such of the booksellers
as maintained circulating libraries.   Bristol had some
of these; poor enough, no doubt, but still contain-
ing books, books, the books for which the poor soul
strove like one fighting for air in a dungeon.   He
had a small allowance of pocket-money, a few pennies
weekly, and as a rule these went straight to the circulating libraries.   Not always, for he had one other
extravagance, and though it arose from the strongest
trait in his character, it has been overlooked by most
of his biographers.   It is quite true that this boy
that has been so bitterly assailed had one wasteful
habit.   The Drawbridge in front of Colston's was
often thronged with beggars and whenever he passed
he emptied his pockets among them.   Even if he
had started to the circulating library to get some of his
beloved books, at the sight of a beggar he surrendered
his last penny and sacrificed his dearest joy.   He was

himself almost as poor as any other person in Bristol, he was himself on the sharp edge of utmost penury, and he gave everything he had, everything even to his books. A kinder heart never beat; at any sight of distress he ran with tears and cries of tenderness to the help. His mother had a friend, a Mrs. Edkins, who had been in her girlhood a pupil of the elder Chatterton's, a warm-hearted, gentle and simple soul, to whom all the Chattertons were dear. She was fond of walking and talking with Thomas, albeit she probably understood little of his sayings. Though poor enough herself, being of the same humble class to which the boy belonged, she sometimes had a little money. Often when they were abroad together, and he had given all his own pennies to some cripple, he would beg her to further his charities. "If you give to the cripple you are giving to me," he told her. When she had intended to round their excursion with a treat of gingerbread or some such rare delicacy, she found herself with empty pocket. Chatterton had insisted that she should give all to the beggars. The moralists have dwelt much upon the fact that to an arrogant pewterer this boy gave a fictitious heraldry. They have not mentioned the other fact that, underfed and poor and joyless himself, he gave bread to the starving. Charity seems to cover all sins but those of the Literary Forger.

I have no idea how much his little philanthropies

and the kindness of his young heart were known, but possibly they had been observed by one man in Bristol of whom, I should say, we have too little information. One of the circulating libraries in Bristol was kept by a bookseller named Goodal, near a place with the euphonious name of the Cider House Passage. To this shop Chatterton was a frequent visitor. Sometimes, after he had shared his book-money with his friends the beggars, he would still stroll on to Goodal's shop to feast his eyes on the books now beyond his reach, and Goodal would take pity on him and put a book under his arm and tell him to run home and not to mind about the fee if he did not have it. In this bitter story of cruelty and neglect you will find few instances where anybody was kind to this boy. Perhaps it is well to make the most of those you do find.

Other persons than the bookseller might have thought him worth attention and for other reasons than his compassionate ways. For his fine face, for one; and then the peculiar uniform of Colston's school notably became him, the dark blue coat, long and full-skirted, the dark blue knee-breeches, yellow silk stockings, low shoes with buckles, round flat blue hat with a gathered brim. You may see boys in the like garb threading the streets of Bristol now,[1]

---

[1] St. Elizabeth's Hospital boys. The costume is almost identical with the old-time Colston uniform.

and if you do you will turn to look at them. And
this boy had that manly bearing and quiet easy address that is rare in boys and immensely engaging
when you do find it. He had no shyness; his manner
towards his elders was always as of one at ease and
confident. Some persons are without the observing
faculty and cannot tell five minutes afterward whether
one that has spoken to them was commonplace or
extraordinary; but wherever was a ready understanding Thomas Chatterton was noted and wondered
over, particularly for those strange eyes of his.
Some of his acquaintances, the surgeon Barrett for
one, used to find entertainment in arousing his anger
to see his eyes burn, a witless device that seems a
kind of grown-up edition of the infant and the watch.
When he was aroused the gray eyes sparkled and
glowed and seemed to take fire from within.

His Saturday half-holidays from twelve to seven
he spent at his mother's house; at seven the doors
of Colston's closed upon him. In these hours at
home he was often busy in the garret, which he had
erected into a study and workshop. There he took
his books and some other things. He kept this den
locked, carried the key himself and would allow no
intrusion upon his privacy. His business in life was
to work. He had made for himself certain wise
adages with which he regaled his mother when that
good woman attempted to remonstrate with him

about his abnormal habits of study and his unboyish disregard of the dinner hour. One was that "God had sent his creatures into the world with arms long enough to reach anything if they chose to be at the trouble." Another about eating animal food was that he had a work to do and must not make himself duller than God had made him. The poor woman, like King Claudius, could make nothing of these answers; the words were not hers. The boy was so affectionate and kindly that she could think no ill of him, but his way of life was beyond her conception and her gossips'.

Later in life Chatterton became an undisguised skeptic as to all revealed religion, but in his early years he was rather devout. He was confirmed when he was ten years old, and the ceremony made a deep impression upon a mind susceptible to all things beautiful and interested in all things ritualistic. He went home from the church to talk to his sister about it and tell her the thoughts it aroused in him. While the mood remained he wrote the earliest of his poems of which we have knowledge, for one of the deplorable as well as the strange features of this story is that so many of its memorials were allowed to perish. Probably he had written many poems before this, as certainly he wrote many after it, that have vanished from the eyes of man. He was ten years old, November 20, 1762, and on January 8, 1763, this poem of his appeared in Felix Farley's *Bristol Journal*:

ON THE LAST EPIPHANY, OR CHRIST COMING TO JUDGMENT

Behold! just coming from above,
The judge, with majesty and love!
The sky divides, and rolls away,
T'admit Him through the realms of day!
The sun, astonished, hides its face,
The moon and stars with wonder gaze
At Jesu's bright superior rays!
Dread lightnings flash, and thunders roar,
And shake the earth and briny shore;
The trumpet sounds at heaven's command,
And pierceth through the sea and land;
The dead in each now hear the voice,
The sinners fear and saints rejoice;
For now the awful hour is come,
When every tenant of the tomb
Must rise, and take his everlasting doom.

His next poem of which we have record, "A Hymn for Christmas Day," written in the same year, 1763, is an amazing composition for a boy ten or eleven years old, showing thought and command of expression, and what is more significant, the sense of music. It begins:

Almighty Framer of the Skies!
O let our pure devotion rise,
  Like incense in Thy sight!
Wrapt in impenetrable shade
The texture of our souls was made
  Till Thy command gave light.

> The sun of glory gleamed, the ray
> Refined the darkness into day,
>   And bid the vapors fly:
> Impelled by His eternal love,
> He left His palaces above
>   To cheer our gloomy sky, *etc.*

It is strange that a boy of such habitual gravity of thought should have also been the possessor of an exquisite sense of humor and a light touch on comic fancy. Not long after his religious hymns appeared he tried his hand at humorous verse, with other things, and produced the beginning of a witty story called "Sly Dick," a tale of a thief in which, if it had been completed, he probably purposed some satire. The next of his preserved writings is "Apostate Will," written when he was eleven years and five months old. The subject is a man that had turned to Methodism and back to the Established Church as advantage dictated, a theme that suited the boy's bent of mind for he had then traveled some distance towards skepticism. Thus the verses begin:

> In days of old, when Wesley's power
> Gathered new strength by every hour;
> Apostate Will, just sunk in trade,
> Resolved his bargain should be made;
> Then straight to Wesley he repairs,
> And puts on grave and solemn airs, *etc.*

I quote a little of it merely to show the lad's peculiar ease in versification and some of the effects that Colston's had already wrought upon him, a contempt for "trade," for instance. It has been generally overlooked that the influence of the school was doubtless responsible for his earliest distaste for religion. Among the iron-bound rules of the institution were severe requirements about worship. Colston had been not less than a fanatic on the subject; not only was his school to be conducted by men of the extremest type of his own faith, but no boy could be admitted that was tainted anywhere with the breath of abhorred dissent, and minute instructions were left as to the kind and quantity of religious faith to be inculcated. Chatterton had much of the rebel in him; he revolted at the idea of being taken by the throat and crammed with dogma, and naturally he sprang away to the other extreme.

The origin of one of his poems of this period shows how keenly he observed current events and how sharp were the powers of sarcasm at his command. One Joseph Thomas, a brickmaker, was then churchwarden of St. Mary Redcliffe. In an inspiration of what was regarded as excessive thrift he ordered that the ground in the churchyard should be leveled off, the grave mounds cut down, and the resulting débris carted off, to his works (as Bristol believed) to be made into bricks. The towns-

people were not unduly sensitive; they had allowed
the Dean of the Cathedral to demolish the old High
Cross in College Green, a beautiful relic of antiquity;
but about the sordid meanness of the churchwarden's
performance there was something that stung. An
outcry was made, people protested, the outraged
feelings found vent in the Englishman's ready resort,
the agony column of his nearest newspaper. Bristol
had not in years been so moved. Thomas, a head-
strong man, was not to be diverted from his purpose
and the work went on to the scandal and wrath of
the town. In the midst of the discussion this boy
of the charity school sprang to the front with a string
of satirical verses, fiercely assailing and lampooning
Thomas and turning upon him a bitter irony by
representing him, extravagantly, no doubt, as tortured by conscience. In his mania for destruction,
the churchwarden, following the vile example of the
Dean, had ordered a cross in the churchyard to be
removed, a merely wanton vandalism that had aug-
mented his other offenses, and the verses picture
him dreaming and gloating over this sacrilege when
the apparition of conscience appears to torment
him. Under the title of "The Churchwarden and
the Apparition," these verses were printed in Felix
Farley's *Bristol Journal*, January 7, 1764, Chatterton then being twelve years old. Like all his
early work they were printed anonymously, and no

one in Bristol would have been more astonished than the editor of that fashionable periodical to find that their author was a little Colston's boy. In the same newspaper appeared a prose philippic on the same subject, and a certain peculiar note of biting satire as well as other internal evidence identifies this also as Chatterton's work. No one else felt so keenly about the desecration. The churchwarden struck at his very heart when he touched St. Mary Redcliffe.

It was so about all things great or small connected with that dear home of his dreams, and presently one of those trifling incidents that turn the currents of life arose from this feeling to the shaping of a new activity and one destined to cause him infinite injury before the unthinking. At Colston's the parchments from the old Muniment Room had long passed from his mind; but being at home one Saturday afternoon he saw his mother winding thread upon an odd-looking slip of paper and asked about it. The answer recalled the whole story of Canynge's Coffer, the abstracted parchments and the handy book-covers. He hesitated not to denounce his father's action as sacrilegious and to declare that nothing old and from the church should be put to base uses. Thereupon he desired to see more of the parchments, and finding them covered with ancient writing fell to studying them. In the end he gathered all that were left in the house, locked them in his garret den and gave orders concerning them in the manner befitting a young gentleman of twelve that was head of a household. Before this he had often been busy of a Saturday afternoon with his drawings and colorings. He had a great lump of ocher, some lampblack and some lead-powder, and with these he worked away, drawing armorial bearings and other devices and coloring them after his fancy, for he had a natural taste for design. From these employments he emerged grimy with lampblack and stained with ocher, but happy. Sometimes he was so much absorbed in his work that he resolutely declined to come down to supper and trudged away back to Colston's that night, hungry but contented. Once he found that having left out of his room his precious bottle of lead-powder, the stuff had been used to polish a stove, and at that he flew into a violent rage, for it was attacking him on two sides, his slender means and his respect for his art. Mainly he drew designs for imaginary castles, ancient bridges and medieval costumes, coloring them; but some time after the incident about the parchments he became busier than ever with his pigments and in other ways.

He was busier also with his pen and more absorbed in his dreams; he had far greater things in mind now than "Apostate Will" and "The Churchwarden," he had things to which all he had done was nothing; he had the expression and artistic flowering of his passionate love for the past wherein he truly dwelt, the expression of Canynge, Rowley, and St. Mary Redcliffe, his inseparable companions of old time. Within him the Grand Romance was taking artistic shape, as slowly he forged its eventual form.

It was inevitable that such a spirit, so utterly possessed of such a story, living in it and brooding upon it, should some day leave a record of it. Probably he had little volition in the matter; the artist can hardly choose, and this was the high aspiring and burning soul of an artist. With all the relics of Canynge about him, with the church, the effigies, the legends that pertained to the sexton's office, the remnant of the Red Lodge, the spire of St. John's Church, with these insistent reminders of truth and fiction, feigned images that had been the companions of his childhood grew upon him as verities, and their deeds took on additional substance. By so much as the Bristol of his own day seemed sordid and mean, by so much as the school he loathed was narrow and dull, the contrast of this imaginary life in a golden age and the contrast of its warm and pleasing figures laid the stronger hold upon his imagination.

In his long lonely rambles, in his long nights in the dormitory (for he slept little), persons and events and at last the whole story had been formulated.

And being now deep in his poetic studies, feeling and knowing exultantly in every fiber that he was a poet, confident of his calling, expert in the characters of ancient writing, a student of heraldry and history, it seemed to him that he knew the poetry that Rowley had made, and he turned back to his old authors, to Spenser and to Chaucer and to an ancient dictionary, to see how the words Rowley had used would look. And having then the spirit and being consumed by the feeling of his creation, presently he began to carve exquisite poetry that he wrote as he thought Rowley might have written. And upon such work, forming on the whole the most extraordinary body of verse in our language, he was then, at the age of twelve years or so, busily engaged. A hard-driven charity school boy, crammed with commerce nine hours a day, set down in an environment that was abhorrent to him, whipped by the head-master (a blockish person named Warner) for wasting his time in such nonsense as poetry, he was steadily building the Rowley fabric into the shape that was presently to amaze the world.

The loneliest soul that has walked these ways of ours, there was in all the world not one person to whom he could impart these transports. Sympathy is as much as air a necessity of life. He was starved for the lack of it. As a little boy he had been whipped for reading and hunted with reproaches from his dreaming place by Canynge's tomb. And now he had been beaten again for practising his elected art. His soul told him that what had been called his offenses were morals; his punishments had been the irradicable crimes. The world had been bitter to him. Both from experience and by infallible instinct he understood what cold jeers and rude jests, worse than blows, would beat upon him at any mention of his Rowley dreams. He crept away, as some hurt animals creep, into holes and lonely corners and shared his rapture of creation with Canynge and Rowley, for these would not laugh nor sneer, these had no wounds nor blows to give. And for all else he was alone. There was not one soul to give him counsel or help; if he had been the final being on a dying planet he could not have been a more solitary figure.

For what he did next the wise world has long crucified him; it is so easy to condemn for one error, so hard to remember that every evil dangles on a long chain of evil cause and evil effect. Was it so great a matter, and he twelve years old, fatherless and unfriended? He had sung with the ineffable joy of the artist, soaring among the clouds, a companion of stars and winds, songs that were for him the embodiment of the soul of his Rowley and of his own. And having done this, and remembering the parchments in his mother's house and the antique writing, it occurred to him that Rowley's songs should have a setting of their own times. He therefore cleaned some of the parchments, and in the antique penmanship that he had studied and learned to imitate he copied some of the poems thereon.

It was with these employments that he was now chiefly concerned on his half-holidays in his garret study. His mother's wonder grew upon her. Other boys were not like this, but played or gathered about and delighted in noise. The strangeness of it alarmed her; good soul, to be unusual was clearly evil, and she set herself to find out what all this meant. It was too late, the boy had drawn too far within himself. Once she undertook to destroy a piece of the parchment, but he raised so violent an outcry that she was affrighted and stopped. Once he stood upon a piece of his work to prevent her from taking it. In the end she gave up the attempt and left him to his own devices, being doubtless wise therein and the gainer; for thereafter she and Mary knew more than any other person about his work; and yet these, you will understand, were not confidants to advise or guide him. They gained, in truth, but a new assurance that Thomas was wonderfully active and able and loved them devotedly.

But he did at times exhibit some fruits of his labors. One of the boys at Colston's, himself afterward a stumbling follower of the Muses and exceedingly jealous of his fellow-student, was James Thistlethwaite. He likewise, and under the inspiration of Phillips, had developed other interests than the multiplication table. One day in July, 1764, a holiday it was, Thistlethwaite, going down Horse Street, near the schoolhouse, encountered Chatterton going up. They were not very friendly. Thistlethwaite was a priggish sort of boy, with a hard angular mind, and Chatterton had an antipathy to prigs. They stopped and talked, nevertheless, and Chatterton announced that he had a piece of news. He had been examining some old parchments taken from St. Mary Redcliffe and had found among them an ancient poem. Thistlethwaite naturally wished to see it. Chatterton said he had given it to Phillips, the usher. Soon afterward Thistlethwaite meets Phillips, the usher, and asks him about this wonder of a by-gone age. Phillips produces it and there it is, a little piece of yellowish parchment, much stained as if by age, and on it some strange old writing, very small and dim. Phillips has been tracing the letters over with his pen to make them clearer. Bit by bit he has made out some words, but others still baffle him. Thistlethwaite sits down with him and together they labor. It is all too much for Thistlethwaite's poor head, but he can see it is poetry, although it is written in the manner of prose, that is without capitals and without division into lines. What Phillips deciphered stuck in Thistlethwaite's memory, and years afterward he recognized the whole poem when he saw it worked out and in print. It was a kind of eclogue called "Elinoure and Juga," and this was its first stanza as it read when it had been recast into lines:

Onne Ruddeborne bank twa pynynge Maydens sate,
Theire teares faste dryppeynge to the waterre cleere;
Echone bementynge for her absente mate,
Who atte Seyncte Albonns shouke the morthynge speare.
The nottebrowne Elinoure to Juga fayre
Dydde speke acroole, wythe languishment of eyne,
Lyche droppes of pearlie dew lemed the quyvryng brine, *etc.*

A little labor would have made this into excellent verse, as follows:

On Rudborne bank two pining maidens sat,
Their tears fast dripping to the water clear,
Each one lamenting for her absent mate,
Who at Saint Albans shook the murdering spear.
The nutbrowne Elinor to Juga fair
Held crooning plaint with heavy cast-down eyne;
Like drops of pearly dew gleamed the quivering brine, *etc.*

But neither Phillips nor Thistlethwaite was concerned in the poetic significance of the composition, and only Phillips cared about it even as a curiosity. The seven stanzas of the poem recited the alternate complaints of the maidens whose lovers were fighting in the War of the Roses, all spirited and justly framed. Phillips seems to have made little of it.

This was the first glimpse we have of Chatterton's secret labors and indicates that he already had his romance well in hand and had found what seemed to him from his readings and from probability to be the language in which Rowley wrote. He was then really less than twelve years of age. The world cherishes stories of precocious achievements by many of its accepted favorites, by Pope, Macaulay, Keats, Bryant, Shelley; among them all is no fellow to this.

IV

THE TRADE OF A SCRIVENER

HE was almost seven years at Colston's, continuing vigorously in his self-appointed tasks, as in those imposed upon him, reading everything in the shape of a book he could lay hands upon and observing with a discerning eye and a singularly retentive memory the ways of men and tides of events. His career in the school seems to have been to the satisfaction of the teachers, although he had no love for the head-master, who had beaten him for writing poetry, and none for the institution. In July, 1767, he being then fourteen years and eight months old, the school authorities held him to be sufficiently trained to be articled, and he was accordingly apprenticed to John Lambert, a dry, formal lawyer, of Bristol, to learn the trade of a lawyer's scrivener. Lambert paid to the trustees a premium of ten pounds. The articles provided that he should feed, lodge and clothe his apprentice; Mrs. Chatterton was to see to her son's mending.

At Lambert's, at first in St. John's Steps, and later in Corn Street, in an old house not long ago demolished,

Chatterton took up his quarters, feeling somewhat aggrieved because Lambert's mother, old, exacting, and of a mind to be a domestic tyrant, made him eat in the kitchen and sleep with the foot-boy. His work was of the easiest. He had little to do but to keep the office in order, to occupy it in Lambert's absence and to copy precedents. From eight to ten every evening was time he had to himself. The leisure his scanty employment gave him he turned to his studies and to his poetry. Of these pursuits Lambert heartily disapproved, favoring his apprentice with stern lectures against idleness and folly (of which he conceived the writing of poetry to be a conspicuous example), and once proceeding to even more violent reproof. Chatterton cherished a bitter resentment against Head-master Warner, who had beaten him for practising his dearest employments, and having now leisure and opportunity, he wrote out his candid opinion of his late preceptor and sent it to him. The literature of caustic abuse is probably the poorer by the disappearance of this effusion, for judging by the results it must have been of a powerful and searching eloquence. Chatterton having abstained from signing his name to the document, Warner, who seems to have been of a breadth and dignity of mind then not uncommon in men of his profession, set in motion much ponderous machinery to discover his correspondent; and when by tracing the kind of paper used this was found to be a boy not fifteen years of age, Lambert met the requirements of the crime by beating him again. From these beatings and repressions there came forth finally a deception at which many sage moralists have been pleased to wonder, being apparently of the belief that from the thistles of tyranny and brutality should come the figs of a sweet and child-like innocence. This boy was born with an abnormally sensitive soul, a mind that soared above his surroundings, and with the artist's irrepressible passion for expression. But when that passion struggled up and took the only shape possible for his genius, and when the aspiring soul had its own flowerage of song, it earned only the cudgel. He was a mere slip of a lad, thin from long fasting and sleeplessness (for his way of living was like an anchorite's), undersized and sensitive, and when the surging fire within him burst forth, men beat him for it. They beat him yet. In Bristol the trouble was that he wrote poetry and let it be known; since then he has been condemned because he wrote poetry and kept it secret. Even the sympathetic among the commentators have seemed to think that the cudgel should breed candor and beatings inculcate frankness. He was a child, without experience, without a close friend or adviser, and it is held, apparently, that the injustice he suffered and the hardships of his incongruous position he should have borne with the calm resignation of an aged saint.

He knew perfectly well in that strange strong mind of his that grown men had no right to beat him for writing poetry. He knew perfectly well that he was different from the people about him, that he had other ideals of life and other aims, that he knew more than most adults, that his mental processes were surer and quicker. He could think and most of them could not. But they had the stronger physical force and could beat him at will and make him waste his precious hours in grinding the sand of commercial arithmetic and copying the dull lawyer's dull precedents. And they would not see that he could do anything else, that there was in him the fire of great achievement. From the seeds of such conditions the growth that came is the last that should astonish reasonable men.

He had, not long after the incident of the Warner letter, a chance to amuse himself at the expense of his tormentors, and availed of it in a way quite natural to the consciously superior mind. The principal crossing in the harbor is and has been for centuries known as "Bristol Bridge." When Chatterton was born this was that ancient stone structure having houses on each side to which I have before referred. Age having impaired the old bridge the authorities in 1768 replaced it. The new bridge

The Bristol Bridge, that was Built in Chatterton's Time.

(From an old water-color in the Bristol Museum.)

was opened to foot passengers in September and completed two months later. While the subject still occupied the minds of the citizens, those that read Felix Farley's *Bristol Journal*, were astonished one day to find printed there what purported to be an authentic account, taken from an ancient manuscript, of the ceremonies that three hundred years before had marked the opening of the old bridge. The account, which would make about one third of a column in a modern newspaper, was most circumstantial and full of minute detail. It was written in what was accepted by the scholarship of that day as veritable old English.

"On Fridaie," it began, "was the time fixed for passing the newe Brydge: Aboute the time of the tollynge the tenth Clock, Master Greggorie Dalbenye mounted on a Fergreyne Horse, enformed Master Mayor all thyngs were prepared; whan two Beadils want fyrst streyng fresh stre, next came a manne dressed up as follows — Hose of goatskyn, crinepart outwards, Doublet and Waystcoat also, over which a white Robe without sleeves, much like an albe, but not so longe, reeching but to his Lends: a Girdle of Azure over his left shoulder, rechde also to his Lends on the ryght, and doubled back to his Left, bucklyng with a Gouldin Buckel, dangled to his Knee; thereby representyng a Saxon Elderman. — In his hande he bare a shield, the maystrie of Gille a

Brogton, who paincted the same, representyng Saincte Warburgh crossynge the Ford. Then a mickle strong Manne, in Armour, carried a huge anlace; after whom came Six Claryons and Six Minstrels, who sang the Song of Saincte Warburgh; then came Master Maior, mounted on a white Horse, dight with sable trappyngs, wrought about by the Nunnes of Saincte Kenna, with Gould and Silver; his Hayr brayded with Ribbons, and a Chaperon, with the auntient arms of Brystowe fastende on his forehead. Master Maior bare in his Hande a gouldin Rodde, and a congean squier bare in his Hande, his Helmet, waulking by the Syde of the Horse: than came the Eldermen and Cittie Broders mounted on Sable Horses, dyght with white trappyngs an Plumes, and scarlet copes and Chapeous, having thereon Sable Plumes; after them, the Preests and Freeres, Parysh, Mendicaunt and Seculor, some syngyng Saincte Warburgh's song, others soundyng clarions thereto, and others some Citrailles. In thilk manner reechyng the Brydge, the Manne with the Anlace stode on the fyrst Top of a Mound, yreed in the midst of the Bridge; then want up the Manne with the Sheelde, after him the Minstrels and Clarions. And then the Preestes and Freeres, all in white Albs, makyng a most goodlie Shewe; the Maior and Eldermen standyng round, theie sang, with the sound of Clarions, the Song of Saincte Baldwyn; which beyng done, the Manne on the Top threwe with greet myght his Anlace into the see, and the Clarions sounded an auntiant Charge and Forloyn: Then theie sang againe the songe of Saincte Warburgh, and proceeded up Chrysts hill, to the cross, where a Latin Sermon was preeched by Ralph de Blundeville. And with sound of Clarion theie agayne went to the Brydge, and there dined, spendyng the rest of the daie in Sportes and Plaies, the Freers of Saincte Augustine doeyng the Plaie of the Knyghtes of Bristowe, and makynge a great fire at night on Kynwulph Hyll."

The intellectual life of Bristol at that day was not remarkable, but there were some persons sufficiently interested in antiquities to be aroused to curiosity by this extraordinary document, and inquiries were set on foot to discover the original. It appeared that the publisher of the *Journal* held no knowledge of it, pursuing a pleasing practise of printing what was sent to him and asking no questions. The signature to the note that accompanied the account was "Dunhelmus Bristoliensis," which threw no light on the mystery. For some weeks the aroused antiquarians of Bristol were baffled in their search. Then a slender youth entering the *Journal* office with a communication to be published was recognized by some one there as the purveyor of the "Dunhelmus Bristoliensis" manuscript and was detained and questioned. Being but a lad and this being Bristol, where, it seems, boys were but troublesome beasts, his examiners went at him hammer and tongs with threats and stern aspect. Whereupon the boy drew himself up haughtily, turned upon them two blazing eyes and refused to utter a word about the manuscript. A symptom of sense returning to some of the interlocutors, he was approached in another way and as if he might possibly be a reasonable being. Meeting, as was his wont, courtesy with courtesy, after some persuasion, he said that the original document was one of a mass of old parchments taken by his father from the Muniment Room of St. Mary Redcliffe; and with this statement the aroused antiquarians of Bristol were, singularly enough, content. At least they did not demand to see the original, made no inquiries about other documents that might exist in the same collection, and desisted from what to the average mind interested in such matters would seem an exceedingly alluring scent. The boy was Thomas Chatterton.

One man in Bristol might easily have surmised the authorship of the ancient story about the opening of the bridge. Surgeon Barrett, if he had stopped to think, might have perceived that his strange boy friend, who talked so much about St. Mary Redcliffe and the ancient things of Bristol, who was so ready and ingenious, would be likely to know something about that peculiar document. But if Barrett suspected the identity of "Dunhelmus Bristoliensis," he confided his thinkings to no one but let that mystery take its course. Yet he now became more intimate than ever with the Blue Coat boy, to whom about this time he was the means of introducing another acquaintanceship [1] almost as unfortunate as his own. Among the surgeon's close cronies was a foolish prating person named George Catcott, of whom we shall hear more, a mindless man whose business was making pewter and who entertained himself with the notion that he had a pretty taste in antiquities and old literature. He was, besides, afflicted with two distempers: a desire to meddle and an insatiable craving for notoriety. Of the latter I cite two in-

[1] The time at which Catcott's acquaintance began with Chatterton is, like so many other facts in this story, clouded by the theories and wishes of various commentators and by uncertain testimony. Catcott himself gave no clear account of it. He said that walking in St. Mary Redcliffe one day a friend told him of the wonderful discoveries of ancient poems recently made there by a young man and he thereupon desired to make this young man's acquaintance. Accordingly an introduction followed. If this account be true the friend was of course Barrett. But Catcott goes on to say that almost at once and freely Chatterton gave him a great number of manuscripts of poems in the antique, and as we know that some of these were not produced until later, and as it was not like Chatterton to be so confiding, the whole narrative is under suspicion. When Catcott made his statement what mind he had was probably failing. He knew so little about Chatterton anyway that he did not know that the boy was a posthumous child. In the Bristol Museum are preserved some very curious notes by Catcott made into a volume with a copy of one of Tyrwhitt's editions of Chatterton in which there are repeated attempts to controvert the conclusions of Tyrwhitt as to the genuineness of Rowley. These notes convey a rather painful notion of the poor man's mentality, but they serve to show how unlucky Chatterton was in the persons that had most to do in influencing his life.

stances: when the new bridge was all but completed
he risked his neck and gave five guineas that he
might be the first to ride a horse across it on loose
planks, an infantile clutch at celebrity of which he
was inordinately proud; and he climbed with ropes the
new spire of St. Nicholas church that he might place
under the top stone a pewter plate bearing his name.
He took himself with such seriousness that in all his
life he never supposed it possible any one could laugh
at him, and when in after years he was lampooned
and satirized, uniformly accepted the most caustic
sarcasm for honest praise. In short, a dull pom-
pous man with no more sense of humor than a sheep.
This creature was prodigiously excited about the
"Dunhelmus Bristoliensis" letter and besieged the
newspaper office to find its source. To the day of
his death he never questioned its authenticity; to
him the whole story was sent out of the veritable
past for his own delectation. He talked much with
Barrett about it and eventually warmed that somewhat frigid person into a show of enthusiasm. The
surgeon perceived that here was something available
for that ponderous history of his; the cackling Catcott
was interested in anything that could be manufactured into conversation (in which he dealt at least
as much as in pewter), and the result was that when
they learned that this boy had knowledge of other
parchments they vied with each other in assiduous
attention to him.

Now this boy, as I have pointed out, had a many-sided mind, and his experience at Colston's clerk mill had ground fine the side that was all a keen and hungry observation of men and affairs. He had associated enough with commonplace persons to see that while they floundered he could go straight to the mark. Hence he had a certain self-confidence in dealing with them and a certain amusement in watching their clumsy mental operations. He had learned at Colston's the essential lesson of commerce, the genial practises of material success, the gospel that what men live for is to surpass or out-maneuver other men. He saw plainly enough the fundamental principle of business, the cold selfishness of gain, and he was not imposed upon by the pretenses of morals with which we are pleased to cloak it. The great passion of his inner life, next to his poetry and his dreams, was books; for books he had an insatiable craving. Barrett had a library and was eager to get old documents to use in his history. Thus, without more words on either side, a kind of agreement was reached. Barrett lent books to Chatterton; Chatterton gave to Barrett copies of old manuscripts, and the spurious history thus evolved, the surgeon, with childish credulity, incorporated into his great tome.

Or in this light, at least, the world has elected to regard Barrett's performances. Whoever comes now to original investigation of this strange story will be likely to gain grave doubts of it. Some things about the compact between the boy and the man have never been revealed; some things in the man's conduct sorely need an explanation that, if we had it, would probably pluck out the heart of this mystery. For instance, was Barrett really ignorant that the boy was manufacturing for him spurious evidence? Was he really deceived about the quality of any purported manuscript that was submitted to him? Did the boy really work without suggestion from any one? From Barrett, for a guess? And of these manuscripts that were delivered every week or so to the historian-surgeon how many were genuine and how many were fictitious?

For we know now that not all the parchments that Chatterton produced were covered with his own inventions; some of the documents carried from Canynge's Coffer had genuine historical value; that is apparent from the scraps that have survived. What has become of those whereof we have now no record? That is the first question. From the time they passed into Barrett's hands they seem to have disappeared. What did he do with them? Copies of some of them, memoranda of others, he used in his history. What became of the originals? Barrett lived to see the authenticity of all the Chatterton documents assailed and defended; he never cared to go into the matter of these originals, although he professed to be deeply interested in all antiquities. Can one conceive that an antiquarian could be so indifferent to such documents that in wantonness or neglect he should destroy them?

And this is but a small part of the cloud of doubt that enfolds all this melancholy matter. It is chiefly because of the fabricated documents he gave to Barrett that the name "forger" has been fastened upon Thomas Chatterton. Most of his other experiments in the antique never saw the light until after his death, and even injustice so gross as has been his portion could hardly charge him with posthumous forgery. But are we so sure that he was the responsible forger in the case of the Barrett documents? Everybody has accepted the story, no one has investigated it. Certainly if that drama were to be re-enacted now we should hesitate to condemn any fifteen-year-old boy on such evidence and in such circumstances. For instance, Barrett was Chatterton's most frequent companion; we know that the boy looked upon the man with more respect and confidence than he felt for any other person in Bristol. At one time he desired to study medicine and to be articled to the surgeon; he was almost daily in the surgeon's house. Admitting it to be quite possible that the boy should be willing to deceive and impose upon the man by giving him false documents, it was extremely improbable that the man should be deceived in any such way. Why? Because there was no other person in Bristol, if in England, so well informed as to the difference between genuine old documents and fabricated old documents.

For long before he knew Thomas Chatterton this surgeon had known about that chest in the Muniment Room and its contents. A barber of Bristol, one Morgan, who dabbled in antiquities (incredible as it may seem the educated men of the day despised such studies when related to their own country), had gathered many of the parchments, certainly as early as the pilfering of others by Chatterton's father, and from Morgan's collection Barrett had been a frequent purchaser. He tells us that he obtained from the barber enough of the old parchments to fill a volume. He never tells us what became of them, but this at least is clear and certain, that before Chatterton came into Barrett's life Barrett was expert in the nature of the genuine old documents from Canynge's Coffer. He had handled, examined, purchased and copied hundreds of them, and being by all accounts a thrifty soul, there was no one less likely to be deceived about them. How could he fail to detect Chatterton's imitations? Of such of these as have come to light few are in the least likely to deceive any one that has eyes good enough to see a church by daylight. And here was Barrett, the shrewd bargainer, the canny purchaser of other things of this nature, taken in by what has never taken in anybody else. To be sure many of the documents were genuine, that is true enough, but as to the rest, either Barrett did not look at them with the least attention, or he knew quite well that they were manufactured and was willing to profit in his way by their making. This is the inevitable conclusion. On the whole, perhaps, we are all wrong in our zeal to denounce this boy. Perhaps some of the odium that for more than a century has hung about his name belongs elsewhere. William Barrett was then a mature man; he was dealing with a boy fourteen, fifteen years old, a boy without training or experience. Suppose we cease to castigate the boy "literary forger" and pay some attention to the man that had at the very least abundant reason to know of the forgeries and never made the slightest effort to discourage them. This man was then engaged in writing a work in which the authenticity of his statements was not likely to be questioned. If there be any kind of a history that is wholly apt to escape too curious comment it is one designed for local consumption and flattering to the local vanity. How could he suspect that this boy would ever be the means of throwing a white light upon his book? His heart was set upon acquiring parchments, there is reason to think he was not disposed to be over-scrupulous about them, and when we discover, as we shall further on, that in one of the fabrications Chatterton had Barrett's active assistance, and that in the one deception that has done the boy the most harm he had Barrett's cooperation and advice, we may well suspect that from the beginning the world has been on the track of the wrong offender.

But even if Barrett had no knowledge of the making of the false manuscripts, even if he were inconceivably dull and inordinately gullible and next to sand blind, even if Chatterton were alone responsible, it is still a just conclusion that we have hounded this boy long enough. Many things are to be considered that in the case of any one else, say one not delegated to be an awful example, would have aroused pity and tender consideration; many facts would seem to palliate and obscure the atrocity of his offense. I purpose to go into them fully here because it is chiefly by the citing of these spurious manuscripts that one of the greatest poets and greatest intellects of the world has been kept out of the recognition due to his genius.

We know, as I have before pointed out, that some of the documents Chatterton furnished were not only genuine but of real interest and value. Now Chatterton supplied these documents in return for books, books that were the life of him, books that he must have or perish intellectually. Supposing, therefore, that the fictitious documents were not made at the instance of another, we may believe that so long as he could he delivered the genuine relics. When they failed, the thought of losing his supply of books was more than he could endure, and the repeated demands of the surgeon drove him to the fabricating of other documents as he had made the parchment copy of "Elinoure and Juga"; the success of that innocent excursion inspired the others.

The suggestion is not mine,[1] hence I am the more at liberty to show how reasonable it may be. As to the genuine nature and historical value of some documents from Canynge's Coffer, that is certain enough. One, at least, of the parchments [2] from that ancient repository threw invaluable light upon the very line of inquiry that Barrett was pursuing. For years after the breaking of the locks on the chests the parchments littered the floor of the Muniment Room. In some way one of them came into the possession of John Browning, of Barton, near Bristol,

---

[1] See Professor Wilson's admirable "Chatterton."

[2] Another document from the same source seems to have a singular history. Horace Walpole, in his letter of defense to the Rev. Mr. Cole, relates it, if any dependence can be placed upon Walpole's testimony. He says that an ancient painter's bill that forms the subject of one of the "Anecdotes of Painting" came from St. Mary Redcliffe, where it had been found some years before Chatterton was born, and transcribed for Walpole by Vertue. Walpole tries to create the impression that Vertue, who was something of a poet, was the inspiration of Chatterton, and that the painter's bill stimulated the boy to his pretended discoveries about old-time painters and others.

and from his cabinet after his death was communicated to the Society of Antiquaries. It recorded the gift by Canynge to Redcliffe Church of a new Easter sepulcher and scenic accessories for the presentation in the church of the Mystery of the Resurrection. The date was July 4, 1470, when Master Nicholas Pyttes was vicar of the church. The details of the gift are quaint and most interesting and throw light upon the manner of playing the Mysteries, which were the only form of dramatic entertainment known in that age. A list of the accessories included painted scenery of timber and cloth representing heaven and hell and God arising from the tomb, with other scenes. This notable matter came straight from Canynge's Coffer and doubtless there were others of like moment.

If so, and we knew them, perhaps they would tend to solve one of the riddles of this mysterious affair. For one thing that always puzzles the investigator of the Chatterton story is the boy's astonishing and unaccountable familiarity with facts in the ancient history of Bristol that no one else was acquainted with, and that nevertheless were well authenticated. I will give two illustrations:

The tower of Temple Church is about five feet out of plumb. In one of the Rowleyan documents Chatterton made a reference to the building of this church that would account for the inclination of the tower. A few years after Chatterton's death, the old gates leading to Temple Church, having become decayed, were dug up and, in the excavating, evidence was found that Chatterton's account of the building was perfectly correct, although in his time knowledge about it seems to have been confined to himself.

Again, in one of the manuscripts presented by Chatterton to Barrett was a description of Canynge's house, the Red Lodge, purporting to have been written by Rowley about 1460. The good priest says therein that the Canynge house occupied the site of an older building, a chapel of St. Mathias. "This Chapel," says Rowley (I modernize for the sake of the reader's ease), "was first built by Alward, a Saxon, in 867, and is now made into a Free Mason's lodge, of which I, unworthy, and Master Canynge are brethren." This was printed in Surgeon Barrett's huge tome, and when these matters began to be scrutinized, was regarded as a mere flight of Chatterton's fancy, no one else having heard of such a matter and no testimony anywhere supporting it. Nevertheless, when early in the last century a great part of the remains of the Canynge house was destroyed for the sweet and reasonable purpose of building a floor-cloth factory, the workmen uncovered under it an arched subterranean passage leading from Canynge's house, and the materials of an old building with

Saxon columns. These columns evidently formed the front line of the buried building facing the river. For these facts there can be no explanation except that the boy possessed sources of information not known by the generality of men. He might, therefore, properly enough communicate this knowledge to Barrett. We have just seen an instance where he did this very thing and where the information was quite correct. How many other such instances are buried in Barrett's dull pages we shall never know.

There is still another plea for our compassion and one not to be overlooked. The old verger now at St. Mary Redcliffe, who shows to visitors the Muniment Room and other interesting matters, always concludes his account of Thomas Chatterton by stating his belief that the boy was induced to his impostures "to help his poor mother." At which wise men, schooled in the accepted accounts, smile at the verger's defense and shake their heads. And yet, so complex are all the motives of men that the verger is partly right. This boy had no more compelling impulse than his passionate devotion to his mother and sister. All his dreams of success and future greatness centered about them; they were to share everything. Many times he told them what he planned to do for them, the house he would build for them, the comfort and luxury they should have when he had achieved his fortune. For them he patiently endured the hardships and freezing atmosphere of Colston's, which in his soul he detested. Hour after hour he spent with them building them these castles and happy in the airy structures. He had his plan, he knew his way of life, and books were as necessary to it as blood to his heart. Here were books at this scheming surgeon's. He reveled in them so long as the genuine documents lasted; we may well think that when these failed a dread lest his supply should be cut off was probably more than he could stand.

For books were so hard to get, so hard! We know now that knowledge is the inalienable inheritance of all mankind, that to expect men to grow straight and sound without it is like expecting a tree to grow in a cellar. But in that day it was different, in that day knowledge was looked upon as a dangerous possession for all except the fortunate. The Bristol Museum and Library preserves a record of the pitiable struggles and trials of Coleridge a few years later to get books in that same city, and Coleridge was a man and already marked by fame. What should this boy do, penniless, alone, unknown, friendless and driven implacably by this fierce thirst to know? Mankind provides the conditions that make wrong-doing inevitable and is then pleased to be much amazed that any one should do wrong. On a calm survey of this instance, the only real amazement will be that this boy did nothing worse than palm off his counterfeit antiques upon two foolish men.

For Catcott insisted upon sharing in the unearthed treasures, and indeed he was of that open-mouthed and childish faith that with his pretensions and arrogance a boy of Chatterton's superior mind and cynical wit could hardly withstand the temptation to fool him. No doubt this was not the stern and edifying rectitude that with great wisdom we expect boys of fifteen to display upon all occasions, but it may be thought that more heinous offenses are of record. "There is in the world," remarks Charles Reade, "an animal of no great general merit but with the eye of a hawk for affectations. It is called a boy." Chatterton knew perfectly well that Catcott's antiquarian skill was sheer affectation, that his comments on ancient literature were merely absurd, that the man was a walking humbug. All quick-witted boys have an impulse to play tricks on such pretenders; the learned gentlemen that have overlooked this fact can never have been boys themselves. When, therefore, the ponderous pewterer wanted to see old manuscripts and talked of them with assumed learning, Chatterton obliged him with a few — from his own workshop.

The number of these fabrications with which he favored the surgeon and the pewterer is really not great, though from the noise they have made in the world one would think they were legion. The penwork is cleverly done, that is beyond dispute, but nothing seems stranger than that any one should have been deceived by them; the ocher stains and candle-marks are so obvious that they look more like the experiments and amusements of an idle hour than like serious attempts at imitation. If Barrett did not indeed know more about their origin than he ever confessed there is need of a far more expert defense of his credulity than has appeared.

The boy's diversions with the surgeon and the pewterer he held as something apart from the business of his soul, which was poetry. By this time we should have far outgrown the notions that any human being does anything great or small for one motive, that minds of extraordinary activity and capacity can be expected to be of one order, and that the creative temperament can always be perfectly consistent. Many causes combined to lead Chatterton along a certain way of deception, and not the least, we may suppose, was the fact that the men he fooled thought they were fooling him. Catcott, at least, believed that his young friend had no knowledge of the value of the manuscripts he produced, and the man's lumbering attempts to secure the manuscripts and yet to avoid the incurring of any expense to himself in the getting of them were doubtless sufficiently amusing. The boy's inconsistency in indulging these pastimes when he was already deep in his conception and creation of the Rowley romance and the splendid Rowley poetry is remarkable enough; and yet the two came together shortly. For when he had made a Rowley poem it was inevitable that he should try it upon some one, and here was the avenue open; he tried it upon Barrett and Catcott, and among the ancient manuscripts to which these worthies were soon treated were copies of some of the best of the Rowley series. A boy fifteen years old and unguided could hardly be supposed to have hit upon very advanced notions about the immorality of deceiving those that had tried to deceive him. How much of the blame for his practises in this respect belongs to those that had been charged with the training of his youthful mind? For instance, how about the head-master that had beaten him for writing poetry? How about other beatings and the glacial atmosphere in which his moral virtues were expected to thrive? How do we know that he was ever taught to do better? And what but deceit is the child's inevitable refuge from tyranny? He had borne on his frail little body the marks of many cudgels, but in all his life no one ever addressed him as a reasonable creature when it came to matters of right and wrong. No one ever took him aside and told him that merely as a matter of practical advantage and daily wisdom the straight plain path was the only path. No one ever invited his confidence, no one was ever interested in what vitally concerned him, nobody ever counseled him as a friend.

I dwell at length upon what to most persons will seem a perfectly obvious and adequate defense, because far more space has heretofore been consumed in denouncing Chatterton for deceiving people than in pointing out to the world his marvelous work. As a matter of fact, Chatterton's relations with the surgeon and the pewterer are just as important as the number of times some other boy played truant. His art means much more than his weakness.

Catcott had for partner in his pewtering enterprise one Burgum, an ignorant vain man, who had prospered without education and, as it subsequently appeared, without deserving. It seems that becoming rich he was at great pains to hide, by an affectation of interest in matters of which he knew nothing, the defects of his early training. No one in Bristol made quicker detection of Burgum's pretenses than Chatterton. Possibly, also, he may have had some intuitive perception of the essential flaw in the man's honesty. However that may be, he saw that Burgum was ambitious to clear what was in contemporaneous eyes the social morass of his origin. One afternoon [1] Chatterton walked into the shop of Burgum & Catcott and quietly asked of the head of the firm this little question:

"Do you know that you are descended from one of the oldest families in England?"

"God bless my soul — no! Is that so? How do you know?" cried the astonished pewterer.

"I have seen the records," said Chatterton calmly.

"Let's hear about it," said the delighted man.

Chatterton obligingly produced a document tracing the pewterer's descent from Simon de Seyncte Lyze, earl of Southampton, who had come over with the Conqueror. The good news must have unsettled Burgum's reason, for it is stated that he gave the boy five shillings. The pedigree was carried down as far as the middle of the thirteenth century. In

---

[1] The period of the making of De Bergham pedigree is only one of innumerable matters about which in this story there have been conflicting surmises. Every biographer has fixed the time to suit himself, a genial practise that has prevailed concerning most details connected with Chatterton. Some have made it to occur while Chatterton was a Blue Coat boy and have declared that it was the first of his fabrications and suggested the rest. Joseph Cottle said that it was when Chatterton was sixteen years old, which would mean while he was at Lambert's. One point that all have overlooked is that Barrett assisted in the pedigree, which makes the date later than his introduction to Barrett, and probably at a time when they had long been acquainted. Some of these commentators seem artlessly to assume that Chatterton was of a wide acquaintance in Bristol and knew Burgum as he knew many others. As a matter of fact he knew few persons. Barrett, in all probability, introduced him to Catcott, and through Catcott he became acquainted with Burgum. This would make the hoax on Burgum of a time when Chatterton was in Lambert's office, and show that Cottle, who had no reason to misrepresent the case, had the correct date.

a few days Chatterton returned with another instalment, continuing the family history from one Sir John de Bergham, a famous knight of the thirteenth century, to the reign of Charles II. Sir James de Bergham, said Chatterton's memorandum, "was one of the greatest ornaments of the age in which he lived. He wrote several books, and translated some part of the Iliad, under the title 'Romance of Troy,' which possibly may be the book alluded to in the following 'French Memoire,'" and then follows a quotation in old French. "To give you an idea of the poetry of the age," continues Chatterton in his memorandum of the pedigree, "take the following Piece, wrote by him (John de Bergham) about 1320."

THE ROMAUNTE OF THE CNYGHTE

BY JOHN DE BERGHAM

The Sunne ento Vyrgyne was gotten,
The floureys al arounde onspryngede,
The woddie Grasse blaunched the Fenne,
The Quenis Ermyne arised fro Bedde;
Syr Knyghte dyd ymounte oponn a Stede
Ne Rouncie ne Drybblette of make,
Thanne asterte for dur'sie dede
Wythe Morglaie hys Fooemenne to make blede
Eke swythyn as wynde. Trees, theyre Hartys to shake.
Al doune in a Delle, a merke dernie Delle,
Wheere Coppys eke Thighe Trees there bee,

There dyd hee perchaunce Isee
A Damoselle askedde for ayde on her kne,
An Cnyghte uncourteous dydde bie her stonde,
Hee hollyd herr faeste bie her honde,
Discorteous Cnyghte, I doe praie nowe thou telle
Whirst doeste thou bee so to thee Damselle?
The Knyghte hym assoled eftsoones,
Itte beethe ne mattere of thyne.
Begon for I wayte notte thye boones.

The Knyghte sed I proove on thie Gaberdyne.
Alyche Boars enchafed to fyghte heie flies.
The Discoorteous Knyghte bee strynge botte strynger the righte,
The dynne bee herde a'myle for fuire in the fyghte,
Tyl thee false Knyghte yfallethe and dyes.

Damoysel, quod the Knyghte, now comme thou wi me,
Y wotte welle quod shee I nede thee ne fere.
The Knyghte yfallen badd wolde Ischulde bee,
Butte loe he ys dedde maie itte spede Heaven-were.

As the pewterer naturally could make nothing of
this, his education being limited to English fairly
writ, Chatterton was good enough to send along a
translation, as follows:

THE ROMANCE OF THE KNIGHT

The pleasing sweets of spring and summer past,
The falling leaf flies in the sultry blast,
The fields resign their spangling orbs of gold,
The wrinkled grass its silver joys unfold,
Mantling the spreading moor in heavenly white,
Meeting from every hill the ravish'd sight.

The yellow flag uprears its spotted head,
Hanging regardant o'er its wat'ry bed;
The worthy knight ascends his foaming steed,
Of size uncommon, and no common breed.
His sword of giant make hangs from his belt,
Whose piercing edge his daring foes had felt.
To seek for glory and renown he goes
To scatter death among his trembling foes;
Unnerved by fear they trembled at his stroke;
So cutting blasts shake the tall mountain oak.

Down in a dark and solitary vale
Where the curst screech-owl sings her fatal tale,
Where copse and brambles interwoven lie,
Where trees entwining arch the azure sky,
Thither the fate-mark'd champion bent his way,
By purling streams to lose the heat of day;
A sudden cry assaults his list'ning ear,
His soul's too noble to admit of fear. —
The cry re-echoes; with his bounding steed
He gropes the way from whence the cries proceed.
The arching trees above obscur'd the light,
Here 'twas all evening, there eternal night.
And now the rustling leaves and strengthened cry
Bespeaks the cause of the confusion nigh;
Through the thick brake th' astonish'd champion see
A weeping damsel bending on her knees:
A ruffian knight would force her to the ground,
But still some small resisting strength she found.
The champion thus: "Desist, discourteous knight,
Why dost thou shamefully misuse thy might?"
With eye contemptuous thus the knight replies,
"Begone! who ever dares my fury dies!"

Down to the ground the champion's gauntlet flew,
"I dare thy fury, and I'll prove it too."

Like two fierce mountain-boars enraged they fly,
The prancing steeds make Echo rend the sky,
Like a fierce tempest is the bloody fight,
Dead from his lofty steed falls the proud ruffian knight.
The victor, sadly pleas'd, accosts the dame,
"I will convey you hence to whence you came."
With look of gratitude the fair replied
"Content; I in your virtue may confide.
But," said the fair as mournful she survey'd
The breathless corse upon the meadow laid,
"May all thy sins from heaven forgiveness find!
May not thy body's crimes affect thy mind!"

The memorandum of the pedigree was thickly
sown with marginal references to the authority for
each statement, "The Roll of Battle Abbey,"
"Cotton's Records," "Ashmole's Order of the
Garter, page 669," "Collins," "Thoresby," and
repeatedly "Rowley," being given as the sources of
information. Some of these authorities were of
Chatterton's invention and some were thoughtfully
drafted to do duty for the occasion. The strangest
thing is that in the composing of this ingenious fraud
he had the assistance of Barrett; here, as so often
elsewhere, we encounter that peculiar person in a
way that arouses suspicion. In the memorandum
of the pedigree the translation of the Latin passages
is in the surgeon's handwriting. It is possible, of

course, that he furnished the translation without knowing for what use it was designed, but it is possible only in the sense that any irrational supposition may be said to be possible. Burgum buzzed much about Bristol of his wonderful pedigree. As he was Catcott's partner and Barrett was Catcott's most intimate friend, it is incredible that Barrett should not hear of it if he did not have it brought to him, and, hearing of it, equally incredible that he should not recognize the Latin translation and the use to which it had been put. Yet he said never a word on the subject. If he had told Catcott, Catcott would have told Burgum; but for four or five years Burgum warmed himself, undisturbed and fatuously confident, in the glory of his new-found greatness. Then for some reason, possibly the incredulity of a neighbor or the scoffing of the ribald-minded, he sent the pedigree for verification to the Herald's College, at London, from which it was quickly returned with its spurious nature clearly demonstrated. Burgum survived the shock and possibly found consolation in the operations by which he subsequently won by fraud his partner's entire fortune.

These were by no means the whole of the boy's activities while at Lambert's. One of his friends at Colston's had been the youth Baker, who also seems to have learned from that competent academy some lessons in disingenuousness. Perhaps we should do well to turn some of our investigating energies toward the school to see what was morally amiss there, for assuredly something was wrong. Baker had now emigrated to Charleston, South Carolina, whence he wrote Chatterton that he had fallen in love with a Charleston beauty named Eleanor Hoyland, and knowing something of his former friend's facility in making verses he begged for a supply of a fervent character that he might pass upon Miss Hoyland as his own. Sound the tucket, let the charge begin upon this Baker, deceiver of the unsuspecting, passer of forged notes in the world of meter! Chatterton, whose views of love on his own account were of an exceedingly cynical and irresponsive sort, nevertheless heeded this cry of distress from the wounded and sent a stock of glowing addresses calculated to melt any lady's heart. "To the Beauteous Miss Hoyland," "Ode to Miss Hoyland," "Acrostic on Miss Eleanor Hoyland," and seven poems in different measures each entitled simply "To Miss Hoyland," sufficiently attest Chatterton's laborious zeal for his friend as well as his versatility. How well he succeeded may be guessed from this specimen:

> Amidst the wild and dreary dells,
> The distant echo-giving bells,
> The bending mountain's head;

Whilst Evening, moving thro' the sky,
Over the object and the eye,
   Her pitchy robes doth spread;

There, gently moving thro' the vale,
Bending before the blust'ring gale,
   Fell apparitions glide;
Whilst roaming rivers echo round,
The drear reverberating sound
   Runs through the mountain side;

Then steal I softly to the grove,
And, singing of the nymph I love,
   Sigh out my sad complaint;
To paint the tortures of my mind,
Where can the Muses numbers find?
   Ah! numbers are too faint!

and so on. It appears that he had not only to imagine the inspiration and beauty of the fair one, but the scenery in which she moved, a task that might have daunted an expert.

In these days he was busily engaged on his Rowley poems, but found time to write in another manner a great deal of verse and some prose. The qualities that make a satirist and the qualities that make a poet are commonly and justly regarded as incompatible. Satire requires a nature observant, keen, humorous, addicted to close reasoning; the singing poet must have introspection, melodic gifts and dreams. That is to say, one nature is the opposite of the other. The sharp difference between the two may be seen if we place Pope by Tennyson, or Dryden by Swinburne. But in this boy were strangely united both natures; he was both dreamer and observer, singer and satirist; he had both introspection and observation. One commentator has asserted that every poet is bi-sexual. Here is one clearly bi-natural. With one side of his nature he dreamed of Rowley and Canynge, dwelt in the past, heard old minstrels and saw the pomp and circumstance of medievalism all about him; with the other side he watched the men and manners of his time and from his observations made a series of satiric portraits of contemporaries at least as vivid as anything that Churchill did and often far more vitriolic. Nothing that happened in the nation and was reported in the newspapers escaped his attention. He saw the conflict beginning between the people and privilege, between surviving feudalism and rising democracy, and from natural sympathy and conviction, he threw himself, a mere boy but with the most powerful pen and original genius in England, into the fight for liberty.

Of the documents supplied by Chatterton to meet the persistent demands of Barrett there were in prose certain writings purporting to have been made by Rowley at Canynge's request and describing the state of the arts, or bearing on old Bristol history;

The Supposed Portrait of Chatterton.
(*From a photograph in the possession of Mr. Edward Bell.*)

and in verse two of the finest specimens of Chatterton's genius, "The Parlyamente of Sprytes" and "The Battle of Hastings." "The Parlyamente of Sprytes" was also entitled "A Most Merrie Entyrlude, plaied bie the Carmelyte Freeres at Mastre Canynges hys greete howse, before Mastre Canynges and Byshoppe Carpenterre, on dedicatynge the chyrche of Oure Ladie of Redclefte," "wroten bie T. Rowleie and J. Iscamme," Iscam being in the Rowley romance a canon of St. Augustine's monastery. If we suppose Barrett to have been an innocent dupe he must have been too ignorant to know whether interludes in modern rhymes and elegant stanzas were played in the time of Edward IV and too dull to be suspicious of the appearance of a second medieval poet also of extraordinary endowments, but in simple faith accepted all. He incorporated "The Parlyamente of Sprytes" as a veritable document in his interminable "History of Bristol," if that has any bearing on the question. The piece has an introduction in several stanzas followed by a spirited chorus, and then proceeds, in a manner of a mask (bearing, in fact, considerable resemblance to Mr. Swinburne's "Masque of Queen Bersabe"), the spirits of various worthies coming in with speeches in different stanzas; for one of the most amazing things about this amazing boy is his facility in varying stanzaic and metrical forms, in

which he excels any preceding English poet. In this
brief poem, for instance, there are eight kinds of
stanzas, of which two are wholly of Chatterton's
invention and some others are adapted or changed
for his purpose. The introduction ("Entroductyon
bie Queene Mabbe") begins thus:

> Whan from the erthe the sonnes hulstred,
> Than from the flouretts straughte with dewe,
> Mie leege menne makes yee awhaped
> And wytches theyre wytchencref doe.
> Then ryse the sprytes ugsome and rou,
> And take theyre walke the letten throwe.
>
> Than do the sprytes of valourous menne,
> Agleeme along the barbed halle;
> Pleasaunte the moultrynge banners kenne,
> Or sytte arounde yn honourde stalle.
> Our sprytes atourne theyr eyne to nyghte,
> And looke on Canynge his chyrche bryghte.

This has been partly modernized, not very happily,
for Mr. Skeats, as follows:

> When from the earth the sun's hulstrèd,
> Then, from the flowrets straught with dew,
> My liege men make you awhapèd,
> And witches then their witchcraft do.
> Then rise the sprites ugsome and rou,
> And take their walk the churchyard through.
>
> Then do the sprites of valorous men
> Agleam along the barbed hall,

> Pleasant the moldering banners ken,
> Or sit around in honored stall.
> Our spirits turn their eyes to-night,
> And looke on Canynge's churchè bright.

"Hulstred" means hidden, "straught" is filled or stretched, "awhaped" is amazed, "ugsome" is ugly, "rou" is rough, "barbed" means adorned. Attempts to modernize Chatterton are always unsatisfactory. The antique words of his usage and the words he coined were chosen by him with a musician's delicate sense of sound value; to change them always impairs the harmony. Whoever would know all the worth of Chatterton's poetry must take the slight trouble to read him in the original. He is no harder than Chaucer; in fact I think easier than Chaucer. The chief requirement is to observe a small glossary that might be printed at the bottom of each page, and once the significance of the strange words is learned the verse appears of a wonderful and ethereal quality of beauty. It should be borne in mind also that the general scheme of the Rowley versification is often, like Chaucer's, rhythmical, not metrical. Thus in this introduction the natural readings of the first and third lines (in the way that Chatterton undoubtedly intended), is

> Whan from the erthe the son-nes hulstred

and

> Mie leeg-e menne makes yee awhap-ed.

It is exceedingly difficult to maintain these essential rhythms in any modernized version.

After the introduction and an address to the Bishop of Worcester the "Spryte of Nymrodde" speaks in a four-lined, alternately rhymed stanza, and in a manner exactly reproduced from the old moralities.

> Soon as the morne but newlie wake,
> Spyed Nyghte ystorven lye:
> On herre corse dyd dew droppes shake,
> Then fore the sonne upgotten was I, *etc.*

"Ystorven" means dead. It will be seen by this example that there is nothing very difficult about reading Chatterton after the eye has grown accustomed to the strange spelling of familiar words.

The "Sprytes of Assyrians" then sing a chorus of which the first stanza is

> Whan toe theyre caves aeterne abeste,
> The waters ne moe han dystreste
> > The worlde so large
> > Butte dyde dyscharge
> Themselves ynto theyre bedde of reste, *etc.*

The spirits of eminent men then speak one after another of themselves and their deeds on earth, Elle or Aella, the mythical Saxon lord of Bristol (anciently "Brystowe" or "Bright-stowe"), and hero of some of the Rowley poems, Fytz Hardynge, Knyghtes, Templars, Frampton and others, ending with a second speech by Elle. In these speeches we find for the first time what may be called the Rowleyan stanza, several times used by Chatterton in these poems, consisting of ten lines rhymed as follows: a, b; a, b, b, c; b, c, c, d, d; or, not to use a scheme that may seem too technical, the first line rhymes with the third, the second with the fourth, fifth and seventh; the sixth with the eighth and the ninth with the tenth. We may take for an example of this stanza one from the speech of Fytz Hardynge:

> The pypes maie sounde and bubble forth mie name,
> And tellen what on Radclefte syde I dyd:
> Trinytie Colledge ne agrutche mie fame,
> The fayrest place in Brystowe ybuylded.
> The royalle bloude that thorow mie vaynes slydde
> Dyd tyncte mie harte wythe manie a noble thoughte;
> Lyke to mie mynde the mynster yreared,
> Wythe noble carvel workmanshyppe was wroughte.
> Hie at the deys, lyke to a kynge on's throne,
> Dyd I take place and was myself alone.

A variation of this stanza appears in the first speech of Aella or Elle, wherein is exhibited, by the way, the strong sense for illuminating details, the feature of Chatterton's art that has given him enduring place among the colorists. He was, in fact, a painter, using words for colors.

There sytte the canons; clothe of sable hue
Adorne the boddies of them everie one;
The chaunters whyte with scarfes of woden blewe,
And crymson chappeaus for them toe put onne,
Wythe golden tassyls glyttrynge ynne the sunne;
The dames ynne kyrtles alle of Lyncolne greene,
And knotted shoone pykes of brave coloures done:
A fyner syghte yn sothe was never seen.

A stage like this, bright with colors, and a background of the varied trappings of medievalism, aroused the full strength of his artistic sympathies. He could paint other things well, but these and flowers he painted best. With any suggestion of the times in which his spirit dwelt he was instantly at home. He could see knights and monks, raised dais and banquet hall, charger and plume, castle and banner, not only in a general perspective but with a richness of detail unsurpassed in our literature. It was not enough that he should see the "chaunters" dressed in "whyte"; the picture in his mind is incomplete without the blue scarf, the crimson hat, the gold tassels; and when he comes to the women he observes the ribbon-knots on their shoes as carefully as the colors of their gowns. It is this particularity of detail, and especially of significant detail, that has been noted as the most effective element in the art of two great modern poets, Rossetti and Morris — the power to seize upon and use the particulars that will bring before the mental vision, clear, vivid, veritable, the scene as the poet saw it. Keats, and many others since him, have had this great gift and used it for the delight of generations; but the first conspicuous instance of it in our poetry is to be found in the works of this strange boy of the charity school.

"The Battle of Hastings" has a rather odd history that may serve to show us with what kind of men Chatterton was dealing. Two versions of the poem exist. When Chatterton delivered to Barrett the first version it bore a note under the title that it was "wrote by Turgot, the Monk, a Saxon, in the tenth century, and translated by Thomas Rowlie, parish preeste of St. Johns, in the city of Bristol, in the year 1465." Barrett accepted this without question, but soon afterward thought (belatedly, as it seems), he should like to see some of the originals of all these treasures and asked Chatterton for the manuscript from which he had copied "The Battle of Hastings." Chatterton thereupon admitted that he himself had written "The Battle of Hastings" — for a friend. But he cheered the surgeon with the announcement that he had another poem on the same subject, a copy of an original by Rowley; and Barrett asking him for this second poem, after a time Chatterton gave him version No. 2, with the title "Battle of Hastyngs, by Turgotus, translated by Roulie for

W. Canynge, Esq." In order to accept the theory
that Barrett was an innocent dupe we are obliged
to believe that he saw nothing suspicious in this
extraordinary performance, that he desisted from
his pursuit of the original, that Chatterton's admission of the authorship of the first poem suggested
nothing to the surgeon when another was forthcoming,
that he accepted without question the appearance of
these impossible Saxon poets and modern translators.
One in whom all these things could awaken no sus-
picions would seem unsafe to be at large unattended.
Surely, the force of credulity could no further go.
But Barrett, according to the wonted version of the
story, had decided that Chatterton was stupid, and
the comfortable doctrine is advanced that such a
mind once reaching a conclusion becomes thereafter a very Gibraltar against facts. Years afterward, when all these events had begun slowly to
take their place in the proper perspective and the
literary world was beginning to see how marvelous
a mind had glowed and gone out, Barrett still assured
those that came to Bristol to investigate the story
that Chatterton's talents "were by no means shin-
ing." There is a post-facto flavor to this assertion
that does not seem eminently satisfying, but I give
it for what it is worth.

The first version of "The Battle of Hastings" is
in a ten-line stanza, but different from the stanza

we have previously examined. The course of the battle, or of a battle, is described with a great minuteness to the middle of the sixty-seventh stanza, where the version suddenly breaks off. Two stanzas will suffice to give an indication of its style and quality.

> Duke Wyllyam drewe agen hys arrowe strynge,
> An arrowe withe a sylver-hede drewe he;
> The arrowe dauncynge in the ayre dyd synge,
> And hytt the horse Tosselyn on the knee.
> At this brave Tosslyn threwe his short horse-speare,
> Duke Wyllyam stooped to avoyde the blowe;
> The yrone weapon hummed in his eare,
> And hitte Sir Doullie Naibor on the prowe;
> > Upon his helme soe furious was the stroke,
> > It splete his bever, and the ryvets broke.
>
> .   .   .   .
>
> And nowe the battail closde on everych syde,
> And face to face appeard the knyghts full brave;
> They lifted up theire bylles with myckle pryde,
> And manie woundes unto the Normans gave.
> So have I sene two weirs at once give grounde,
> White fomyng hygh to rorynge combat runne;
> In roaryng dyn and heaven-breaking sounde,
> Burste waves on waves, and spangle in the sunne;
> > And when their myghte in burstynge waves is fled,
> > Like cowards, stele alonge their ozy bede.

If this be not great poetry of its kind there is none in the language.

In the second version, which is written in a different stanza, there is much description of an

inspired order of beauty, and some that shows us
the indebtedness of Keats and a long line of other
colorists. Take for instance these stanzas on
Kenewalchæ, wife of Adhelm, a knight in Harold's
army:

> White as the chaulkie clyffes of Brittaines isle,
> Red as the highest colour'd Gallic wine,
> Gaie as all nature at the mornynge smile,
> Those hues with pleasaunce on her lippes combine —
> Her lippes more redde than summer evenynge skyne,
> Or Phœbus rysinge in a frostie morne,
> Her breste more white than snow in feeldes that lyene,
> Or lillie lambes that never have been shorne,
> Swellynge like bubbles in a boillynge welle,
> Or new-braste brooklettes gently whyspringe in the delle.
>
> Browne as the fylberte droppyng from the shelle,
> Browne as the nappy ale at Hocktyde game,
> So browne the crokyde rynges, that featlie fell
> Over the neck of the all-beauteous dame.
> Greie as the morne before the ruddie flame
> Of Phœbus' charyotte rollynge thro the skie,
> Greie as the steel-horn'd goats Conyan made tame,
> So greie appear'd her featly sparklyng eye;
> Those eyne, that dyd oft mickle pleased look
> On Adhelm valyaunt man, the virtues doomsday book.

Barrett had also the "English Metamorphoses"
purporting to have been written by Rowley, a version in the Rowleyan stanza of the Legend of
Locrine told by Spenser in the "Faerie Queene,"

(and utilized by Mr. Swinburne in his extraordinary rhymed tragedy) relating the myth of the origin of the River Severn's name. It has interest as showing that Chatterton attentively read Spenser, and as exhibiting the facility wherewith he bent his stanza to all purposes, narrative or lyric. But of this we shall see still more remarkable illustrations.

One other of these productions has a more interesting history. In the Rowleyan romance were poems about the same mythical Aella we have before encountered, lord of the castle at Bristol, victor over the Danes in the battle of Watchet, whose mighty deeds Rowley was supposed to sing. Chatterton accordingly favored Barrett with a copy of a "Songe to Aella," as a work of Rowley's. Barrett asked for the original manuscript. The next day Chatterton returned with a piece of parchment on which the poem was written in a clever imitation of the ancient chirography and in the manner of prose without capitals and without division into lines. The ink had the appearance of age and the whole parchment had superficial evidences of antiquity. The writing was small and extremely difficult to make out, but regular and all in keeping. It was noticed that the manuscript contained some variations from the copy that Chatterton had offered the day before, but to the artless Barrett, this fact again seems to have suggested no query. We are to believe he entertained no doubt that he was handling some of the veritable handiwork of Thomas Rowley, preserved through centuries in the Muniment Room of St. Mary Redcliffe to adorn at last the History of Bristol.

"Songe to Aella, Lorde of the Castel of Brystowe ynne Daies of Yore," it is called.   It begins thus:

> Oh thou, orr whatt remaynes of thee,
>   Aella, the darlynge of futurity,
> Lett thys mie songe bolde as thie courage be,
>   As everlastynge to posteritye.
> Whanne Dacya's sonnes, whose hayres of bloude redde hue
> Lyche kynge-cuppes brastynge wythe the morning due,
>   Arraung'd ynne dreare arraie,
>   Upponne the lethale daie,
> Spredde farre and wyde onne Watchets shore;
>   Than dyddst thou furiouse stande,
>   And bie thie valyante hande
> Beesprengedd all the mees wythe gore.

About the time that Rowley lived in Bristol John Lydgate, author of "London Lyckpenny" and a poet of renown and merit, was dwelling in London. Chatterton, as an ornament to the Rowley tissue that his fancy had woven, imagined his hero to have sent to Lydgate a copy of the "Songe to Aella" and Lydgate to have replied upon Rowley with a metrical epistle of five four-lined stanzas, and this also he conveniently added to the store already in the hands of Barrett.

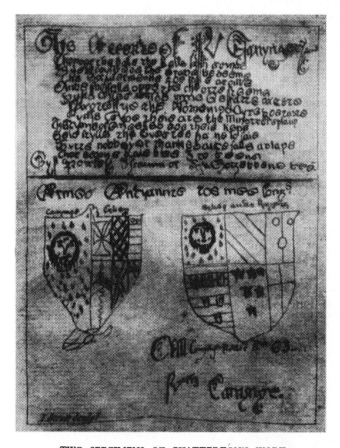

TWO SPECIMENS OF CHATTERTON'S WORK

The first is a photographic copy of the parchment that Chatterton gave to Barrett, purporting to be the original of a poem by Rowley, entitled *The Account of W. Canynge's Feast.* The lines shown above read as follows:

Thorowe the halle the belle han sounde;
Byelecoyle doe the Grave beseeme;
The ealdermenne doe sytte arounde,
Ande snoffelle oppe the cheorte steeme.
Lyche asses.wylde ynne desarte waste
Swotelye the morneynge ayre doe taste.
Syke keene thie ate ; the minstrels plaie,

The dynne of angelles doe theie keepe;
Heie stylle, the guestes ha ne to saie,
Butte nodde yer thankes ande falle aslape.
Thus echone daie bee I to deene,
Cyf Rowley, Iscamm, or Tyb. Gorges be
ne seene.

Beneath are the arms of Canynge as designed by Chatterton. They are not correctly given as the real bearings were three negroes' heads.

The above fac-simile is by the permission of the British Museum, where the originals are preserved. The parchment is artificially discolored to give it the appearance of age, but so carelessly that in one place the original color is plainly to be seen. The writing in the poem is in red ink and so clear that no observant person could fail to see that it is modern. In fact the evidences of recent manufacture are so palpable that it is difficult to imagine how Barrett could be deceived by the imposture.

A particularly fine specimen of his work of these days (about his sixteenth year) is an interlude called "Goddwyn." It begins with this list of the "Persons Represented," from which it will be seen that on this occasion Mr. Canynge enjoyed at the Red Lodge the society of almost the entire company of Rowleyan Sprites:

> *Harolde*, bie T. Rowleie, the Aucthoure.
> *Goddwyn*, Johan de Iscamme.
> *Elwarde*, Syrr Thybbot Gorges.
> *Alstan*, Syrr Alan de Vere.
> *Kynge Edwarde*, Mastre Willyam Canynge.
> Odhers by Knyghtes Mynstrelles.

The form is mostly a ten-line stanza, different from that we have found elsewhere, alternate lines being rhymed usually until the last two, which form a couplet, the tenth line being sometimes an Alexandrine. But there are variations into four, six, and twelve-line stanzas. To give an idea of the spirited manner of this piece I quote the opening lines, using a modernized version, but commending the original to any reader that cares to know what this drama really is. "Loverde" means lord and "aledge stand" means to be molified.

> *God.* Harold!
> *Har.*　　　My loverde!
> *God.*　　　　　　　O! I weep to think
> What foemen rise up to devour the land.

They batten on her flesh, her hearts blood drink,
And all is granted from the royal hand.
Har.   Let not thy grievance cease nor aledge stand.
Am I to weep?   I weep in tears of gore.
Am I betrayed?   So should my burly brand
Depict the wrongs on him from whom I bore.

The subject of the play is the stirring events in the last days of Edward the Confessor and the conspiracy of Goddwyn and Harold to defeat the plans of William of Normandy. There is an amazing skill of character painting in the fragment left us of this play.   Harold is depicted as brave, boisterous, quick-witted and violent, a kind of Saxon Hotspur, but Goddwyn as cold and crafty; and between them the saintly character of King Edward struggles with his inherited blood of battle. The whole thing carried out on the lines begun would have been a notable achievement in any time by any hand. In one place Harold and Goddwyn, one straining forward and the other holding back, are conferring.

God.   Harold, what wouldest do?
Har.   Bethink thee what.
Here lieth England, all her rights unfree,
Here lie the Normans cutting her by lot,
Restraining every native plant to gre.
What would I do?   I brondeous would them sle,
Tear out their sable hearts by rightful breme:
Their death a means unto my life should be,

My sprite should revel in their heart-blood's stream.
Eftsoons I will reveal my rageful ire,
And Goddes anlace wield in fury dire.
God. What wouldst thou with the king?
Har.   Take off his crown:
The ruler of some minister him ordain,
Set up some worthier than I have plucked down
And peace in England should be bray'd again.

Here again I have used Mr. Skeats's moderniz-
ing, which is probably as good as can be made; but
no version can reproduce the strength of the poet's
own work. The piece is broken off in the early
part of the action and still more deplorably in the
midst of one of the loftiest flights of Chatterton's
song and one of the great poems of all times. This
is the famous "Hymn of Liberty" that all critics
have assigned a place with the liberty odes of Shelley,
Coleridge, and Swinburne. As Chatterton wrote it
the swing and impetus of it are irresistible. I
give it here reclothed in modish attire, but do so
reluctantly, looking back to the grace and power
of the first strange words.

When Freedom, drest in blood-stained vest,
To every knight her war-song sung,
Upon her head wild weeds were spread,
A gory anlace by her hung.
She danced upon the heath,
She heard the voice of death.

Pale-eyed Affright, his heart of silver hue,
  In vain essayed her bosom to acale.
She heard, unscared, the shrieking voice of woe,
  And sadness in the owlet shake the dale.
    She shook the burled spear,
    On high she raised her shield,
    Her foemen all appear
    And fly along the field.

Power, with his head up-stretched unto the skies,
  His spear a sunbeam, and his shield a star,
While like two burning balefires roll his eyes,
  Stamps with his iron feet, and sounds to war.
    She sits upon a rock,
    She bends before his spear,
    She rises from the shock,
    Wielding her own in air.

Hard as the thunder doth she drive it on;
  Wit, closely wimpled, guides it to his crown;
His long sharp spear, his spreading shield is gone;
  He falls, and falling rolleth thousands down.
War, gore-faced War, by Envy armed, arist,
  His fiery helmet nodding to the air,
Ten bloody arrows in his straining fist —

And here the great chord breaks off, the music ceases.

Few songs in English will better sustain analysis for consistent design and imagination, and the art of its music is wonderful; it sings itself. The symbolism of Force as the eternal foe of Liberty creeping upon her while she is unaware and being the forerunner of War, and of War springing to arms when by Liberty Force is overthrown, is as effective as has ever been conceived on this subject. What puzzles all judicious readers is that in all these poems there is no sign of an immature or undeveloped power. The lines are forged full strength; nothing falls short of its purpose because of lack of a grasp upon the instrument. How this charity school boy ever came by this facility is a mystery as great as the mystery of Shakespeare.

To Catcott, Chatterton presented several transcripts of what he said were Rowley poems. To see merely the copies of these things seems to have been enough to throw the pewterer into rapturous delight. He never asked to see an original manuscript, never questioned the authenticity of anything, never suspected that he was being gulled, but applauded to the echo each new revelation of Rowley's wondrous skill. Among these treasures was "The Tournament," of which Catcott had a copy in Chatterton's hand-writing. It is a poem sometimes in the Rowleyan ten-line stanza, sometimes in other forms, reciting the prowess of Simon de Burton, the supposed builder of the original church on the site of St. Mary Redcliffe, and, of course, a figure of traditional importance to Bristol. Burton tilts with many knights, including Sir John de Berghamme and finally with the Mysterious Stranger, who had overthrown many other opponents, and all fall before his strength and skill. The thing has dramatic form and much spirit and action, but chiefly is esteemed for the excellent minstrels' song with which it comes to an end after Sir Simon has been crowned king of the tourney:

> Whann Battayle, smethynge wythe new quickenn'd gore,
> Bendynge wythe spoiles, and bloddie droppynge hedde,
> Dydd the merke wood of ethe and rest explore,
> Seekeynge to lie onn Pleasures downie bedde,
>> Pleasure, dauncyng fromm her wode,
>> Wreathedd wythe floures of aiglintine,
>> From hys vysage washedd the bloude,
>> Hylte hys swerde and gaberdyne, *etc.*

which may easily be modernized as follows:

> When Battle, smoking with new quickened gore,
> Bending with spoils and bloody drooping head,
> Did the dark wood of ease and rest explore,
> Seeking to lie in Pleasure's downy bed,
>> Pleasure, dancing from her wood,
>> Wreathed in flowers of eglantine,
>> From his visage washed the blood,
>> Hid his sword and gaberdine, *etc.*

The song is particularly valuable to those that follow the development of English poetry, from its introduction of a trochaic foot (long, short), in the last four lines, the use of troches being very rare before Chatterton's time, and the form followed here, of an iambic alternately with a trochaic movement (iambic in first four lines, trochaic in last four), being without precedent.   Its use in latter-day poems may be seen in Mr. Swinburne's "Litany of Nations" where it appears with powerful effect.

Catcott also came into possession of the "Bristowe Tragedie; or, the Dethe of Syr Charles Bawdin," being a story told in the form of an old ballad and an impressive instance of the boy's fairest work. It has been rightly held to be one of the most powerful ballads we possess.   Some of the pictures in it, as that of the procession, have never been surpassed for clearness and vigor.   I give these extracts in the original form, since the difficulties of reading it are very slight:

> The feathered songster chaunticleer
>   Han wounde hys bugle horne,
> And tolde the earlie villager
>   The commynge of the morne:
>
> Kynge Edwarde sawe the ruddie streakes
>   Of lyghte eclypse the greie;
> And herde the raven's crokynge throte
>   Proclayme the fated daie.
>
> "Thou'rt righte," quod hee, "for, by the Godde
>   That syttes enthron'd on hyghe!
> Charles Bawdin, and hys fellowes twaine,
>   To daie shall surelie die."

Thenne wythe a jugge of nappy ale
  Hys Knyghtes dydd onne hymm waite;
"Goe tell the traytour, thatt to daie
  Hee leaves thys mortall state."

Syr Canterlone thenne bendedd lowe,
  Wythe harte brymm-fulle of woe;
Hee journey'd to the castle-gate,
  And to Syr Charles dydd goe.

But whenne hee came, hys children twaine,
  And eke hys lovynge wyfe,
Wythe brinie tears dydd wett the floore,
  For good Sir Charleses lyfe.

"O goode Syr Charles!" sayd Canterlone,
  "Badde tydings I doe brynge."
"Speke boldlie, manne," sayd brave Syr Charles
  "Whatte says thie traytor kynge?"

"I greeve to telle, before yonne sonne
  Does fromme the welkin flye,
Hee hathe uponne hys honnour sworne,
  Thatt thou shalt surelie die."

"Wee all must die," quod brave Syr Charles,
  "Of thatte I'm not affearde;
Whatte bootes to lyve a little space?
  Thanke Jesu, I'm prepar'd;

"Butt telle thye kynge, for myne hee's not,
  I'de sooner die to daie
Thanne lyve hys slave, as manie are,
  Tho' I shoulde lyve for aie."

Thenne Canterlone hee dydd goe out,
  To tell the maior straite
To gett all thynges ynn reddyness
  For goode Syr Charles's fate.

Thenne Maisterr Canynge saughte the kynge,
  And felle down onne hys knee;
"I'm come," quod hee, "unto your grace
  To move your clemencye."

Thenne quod the kynge, "youre tale speke out,
  You have been much oure friende;
Whatever youre request may bee,
  Wee wylle to ytte attende."

"My nobile leige! alle my request
  Ys for a nobile knyghte,
Who, tho' mayhap hee has donne wronge,
  Hee thoughte ytte stylle was ryghte:

"Hee has a spouse and children twaine,
  Alle rewyn'd are for aie;
Yff thatt you are resolv'd to lett
  Charles Bawdin die to daie."

"Speke nott of such a traytour vile,"
  The kynge ynne furie sayde;
"Before the evening starre doth sheene,
  Bawdin shall loose hys hedde;

"Justice does loudlie for hym calle,
  And hee shalle have hys meede:
Speke, Maister Canynge! whatte thynge else
  Att present doe you neede?"

"My nobile leige," goode Canynge sayde,
　"Leave justice to our Godde,
And laye the yronne rule asyde;
　Be thyne the olyve rodde.

"Was Godde to serche our hertes and reines
　The best were synners grete;
Christ's vycarr only knowes ne synne,
　Ynne alle thys mortall state.

"Lette mercie rule thyne infante reigne,
　'Twylle faste thye crowne fulle sure;
From race to race thy familie
　Alle sov'reigns shall endure:

"But yff wythe bloode and slaughter thou
　Beginne thy infante reigne,
Thy crowne uponne thy childrennes brows
　Wylle never long remayne."

"Canynge, awaie! thys traytour vile
　Has scorn'd my power and mee;
Howe canst thou thenne for such a manne
　Intreate my clemencye?"

"Mie nobile leige! the trulie brave
　Wylle val'rous actions prize,
Respect a brave and nobile mynde,
　Altho' ynne enemies."

"Canynge, awaie! By Godde ynne Heav'n
　Thatt dydd mee being gyve,
I wylle nott taste a bitt of breade
　Whilst thys Syr Charles dothe lyve.

"Bie Marie, and alle Seinctes ynne Heav'n,
　Thys sunne shall be hys laste;"
Thenne Canynge dropt a brinie teare,
　And from the presence paste.

Wyth herte brymm-fulle of gnawynge grief,
　Hee to Syr Charles dydd goe,
And satt hymm downe uponne a stoole,
　And teares beganne to flowe.

"Wee alle must die," quod brave Syr Charles,
　"Whatte bootes ytte howe or whenne;
Deth ys the sure, the certaine fate
　Of all wee mortall menne.

"Saye, why, my friend, thie honest soul
　Runns overr att thyne eye;
Is ytte for my most welcome doome
　Thatt thou doste child-lyke crye?"

Quod godlie Canynge, "I doe weepe,
　Thatt thou soe soone must dye,
And leave thy sonnes and helpless wyfe;
　'Tys thys thatt wettes myne eye."

"Thenne drie the teares thatt out thyne eye
　From godlie fountaines sprynge;
Dethe I despise and alle the power
　Of Edwarde, traytor kynge.

"Whan through the tyrant's welcom means
　I shall resigne my lyfe,
The Godde I serve wylle soone provyde
　For bothe mye sonnes and wyfe.

"Before I sawe the lyghtsome sunne,
  Thys was appointed mee;
Shall mortal manne repyne or grudge
  Whatt Godde ordeynes to bee?

"Howe oft ynne battaile have I stoode,
  Whan thousands dy'd arounde;
Whan smokynge streemes of crimson bloode
  Imbrew'd the fatten'd grounde:

"Howe dydd I knowe thatt ev'ry darte
  That cutte the airie waie,
Myghte nott fynde passage toe my harte,
  And close myne eyes for aie?

"And shall I nowe, forr feere of dethe,
  Looke wanne and bee dysmayde?
Ne! fromme my herte flie childyshe feere,
  Bee alle the manne display'd.

.   .   .   .

"My honest friende, my faulte has beene
  To serve Godde and my prynce;
And thatt I no tyme-server am,
  My dethe wylle soone convynce.

"Ynne Londonne citye was I borne,
  Of parents of grete note;
My fadre dydd a nobile armes
  Emblazon onne hys cote:

"I make ne doubte butt hee ys gone
  Where soone I hope to goe;
Where wee for ever shall bee blest
  From oute the reech of woe:

"Hee taughte mee justice and the laws
  Wyth pitie to unite;
And eke hee taughte mee howe to knowe
  The wronge cause fromme the ryghte:

"Hee taughte mee wythe a prudent hande
  To feede the hungrie poore,
Ne lette mye servants dryve awaie
  The hungrie fromme my doore:

"And none can saye butt alle mye lyfe
  I have hys wordyes kept;
And summ'd the actyonns of the daie
  Eche nyghte before I slept."

. . . .

Quod Canynge, " 'Tys a goodlie thynge
  To bee prepar'd to die;
And from thys world of peyne and grefe
  To Godde ynne Heav'n to flie."

And nowe the bell beganne to tolle
  And claryonnes to sounde;
Syr Charles hee herde the horses' feete
  A praucing onne the grounde:

And just before the officers
  His lovynge wyfe came ynne,
Weepynge unfeigned teeres of woe
  Wythe loude and dysmalle dynne.

. . . .

And nowe the officers came ynne
  To brynge Syr Charles awaie,
Whoe turnedd toe hys lovynge wyfe,
  And thus to her dydd saie:

"I goe to lyfe, and nott to dethe;
　　Truste thou ynne Godde above,
And teache thye sonnes to feare the Lorde,
　　And ynne theyre hertes hym love:

"Teache them to runne the nobile race
　　Thatt I theyre fader runne:
Florence! shou'd dethe thee take — adieu!
　　Yee officers, leade onne."

Thenne Florence rav'd as anie madde,
　　And dydd her tresses tere;
"Oh! staie, mye husbande! lorde! and lyfe!" —
　　Syr Charles thenne dropt a teare.

'Tyll tyredd oute wythe ravynge loud,
　　Shee fellen onne the flore;
Syr Charles exerted alle hys myghte,
　　And march'd fromm oute the dore.

Uponne a sledde hee mounted thenne,
　　Wythe lookes fulle brave and swete;
Lookes, thatt enshone ne more concern
　　Thanne anie ynne the strete.

Before hym went the council-menne,
　　Ynne scarlett robes and golde,
And tassils spanglynge ynne the sunne,
　　Muche glorious to beholde:

The Freers of Seincte Augustyne next
　　Appeared to the syghte,
Alle cladd ynne homelie russett weedes,
　　Of godlie monkysh plyghte:

Ynne diffraunt partes a godlie psaume
  Moste sweetlie theye dydd chaunt;
Behynde theyre backes syx mynstrelles came,
  Who tun'd the strunge bataunt.

Thenne fyve-and-twentye archers came;
  Echone the bowe dydd bende,
From rescue of Kynge Henrie's friends
  Syr Charles forr to defend.

Bolde as a lyon came Syr Charles,
  Drawne onne a clothe-layde sledde,
Bye two blacke stedes ynne trappynges white,
  Wyth plumes uponne theyre hedde:

Behynde hym fyve-and-twentye moe
  Of archers stronge and stoute,
Wyth bended bowe echone ynne hande,
  Marched ynne goodlie route:

Seincte Jameses Freers marched next,
  Echone hys parte dydd chaunt;
Behynde theyre backes syx mynstrelles came,
  Who tun'd the strunge bataunt:

Thenne came the maior and eldermenne,
  Ynne clothe of scarlett deck't;
And theyre attendyng menne echone,
  Like Easterne princes trickt:

And after them, a multitude
  Of citizenns dydd thronge;
The wyndowes were alle fulle of heddes,
  As hee dydd passe alonge.

At the grete mynsterr wyndowe sat
  The kynge ynne myckle state,
To see Charles Bawdin goe alonge
  To hys most welcom fate.

Soone as the sledde drewe nyghe enowe,
  Thatt Edwarde hee myghte heare,
The brave Syr Charles hee dydd stande uppe
  And thus hys wordes declare:

"Thou seest mee, Edwarde! traytour vile!
  Expos'd to infamie;
Butt bee assur'd, disloyall manne!
  I'm greaterr nowe thanne thee.

"Bye foule proceedyngs, murdre, bloude,
  Thou wearest nowe a crowne;
And hast appoynted mee to dye,
  By power nott thyne owne.

.   .   .   .

"Thye pow'r unjust, thou traytour slave!
  Shall falle onne thye owne hedde" —
Fromme out of hearynge of the kynge
  Departed thenne the sledde.

Kynge Edwarde's soule rush'd to hys face,
  Hee turn'd hys hedde awaie,
And to hys broder Gloucester
  Hee thus dydd speke and saie:

"To hym that soe-much-dreaded dethe
  Ne ghastlie terrors brynge,
Beholde the manne! hee spake the truthe,
  Hee's greater thanne a kynge!"

"Soe lett hym die!"   Duke Richard sayde;
  "And maye echone oure foes
Bende downe theyre necks to bloudie axe,
  And feede the carryon crowes."

And nowe the horses gentlie drewe
  Syr Charles uppe the hyghe hylle;
The axe dydd glysterr ynne the sunne,
  Hys pretious bloude to spylle.

Syr Charles dydd uppe the scaffold goe,
  As uppe a gilded carre
Of victorye, bye val'rous chiefs
  Gayn'd ynne the bloudie warre.

.   .   .   .

Thus was the ende of Bawdin's fate:
  Godde prosper longe oure kynge,
And grante hee maye, wyth Bawdin's soule,
  Ynne heav'n Godd's mercie synge!

The boy took this home when he had finished it and with pride showed it to his mother. He told her he had written it, and she never had other belief in the matter; but Catcott instantly ascribed it to Rowley, and despite all the contrary evidence was to the end of his life unshakable in his faith in that authorship.

The oddest thing is that the story the ballad relates is historical, though in all Bristol this boy was probably the only person that knew that fact, and how he found it I do not pretend to say. "Syr Charles Bawdin" is really Sir Baldwin Fulford, a Lancastrian, who was put to death at Bristol in 1461 in the following manner:

In 1460 (according to old Stow, the chronicler) while the War of the Roses was still on, "Richard, Lord Rivers [a Lancastrian], was sent to Sandwich, to keep the town and certain great ships which lay there at anchor; but when the Earl of Warwick saw time convenient he sent some of his men to Sandwich by night, the which took the said Lord Rivers and Anthony Woodville, his son, in their beds, and led them over to Calais, with all the great ships save one called Grace de Dieu, the which might not be had away because she was broke in the bottom. Sir Baldwin Fulford undertook on pain of losing his head that he would destroy the Earl of Warwick." It appears that he went to Calais on this adventure and it failed, and while he was returning home to arouse the people against Edward, who had meantime made great head and been crowned king, he fell into his enemies' hands. He and two squires captured with him were imprisoned in Bristol Castle. When they were brought to trial for high treason one of their judges was William Canynge, who must have served unwillingly in that painful capacity, for the judicial murder of a fellow-adherent of the lost cause was no light matter even in those callous times. All that Edward wanted was to have Fulford put out of the way, and that was quickly achieved. He and the two squires were beheaded almost at once. After the restless charity school boy had passed from the affairs of men it was proved from the old documents of St. Ewin's Church (which was once Bristol Minster), that King Edward was actually in Bristol at the time of Fulford's death. We need not suppose that he went there expressly to attend to the matter of murdering the knight, for he knew that work would be performed by his trusty men, but he was certainly there, the church was cleaned in honor of his visit to it, and from the east window he might have witnessed the procession to the block exactly as Chatterton described. It seems that at the time the "Bristowe Tragedie" was written no one but Chatterton was aware of the king's visit. In the face of such startling facts as these I do not know how any one can with perfect confidence affirm any theory about the Chatterton impostures. He might have found almost anything among those documents that have so mysteriously disappeared from Barrett's hands.

One other thing: His prose protest against the sacrilege of Churchwarden Thomas was signed "Fulford, the Grave Digger." Hence, it is not a forced surmise that he was then familiar with the story of Sir Baldwin Fulford, although he was then only eleven years old.   Given a boy that at eleven knew of the ancient history of his native town more than any graybeard knew and almost anything might be expected when the graybeards imposed upon and beat him.

V

THE RISING FLAME

YET another acquaintance of his in these days and another butt of his secret ridicule was the Rev. Alexander Catcott, vicar of the Temple Church at Bristol, and a brother of the pewterer-antiquarian. Some things the vicar knew, doubtless — Hebrew, for instance, in which he was reputed one of the foremost scholars in England — but he was densely ignorant of the literature of his own country, particularly of its poetry, which he detested, and he was a firm upholder of a literal interpretation of the story of Noah's flood. His faith was no holiday affair: he had endured for it the pains of writing an elaborate book in its defense, and he had a collection he was pleased to call geological from the which he offered to prove his doctrine to the confusion of any skeptic. He had, moreover, certain traits of mind calculated to add to the concealed satisfaction of a cynical observer. He was extremely opinionated, narrow, and bigoted, though doubtless well enough meaning. For a time Chatterton found some pleasure in leading this good man into the interminable bog of theological debate, wherein the rector probably floundered rather amusingly. For himself Chatterton had long made up his mind about religion, and his attitude theretoward was almost identical with the creed that Shelley afterward held. That is to say, he had his own religion of faith and practise, dream and aspiration, but utterly rejected all the dogmas of the church and, indeed, all the supernatural parts of Christianity. He used to go to hear the Rev. Mr. Catcott's sermon of a Sunday morning and tell him in the afternoon how far astray he had been in his logic, a practise to which the defender of Noah's flood was not partial. Previously Chatterton had formed a brief acquaintance with the Rev. Mr. Broughton, rector of his own St. Mary Redcliffe, but Broughton seems to have been irritated by the boy's frankly delivered opinions; they soon quarreled and Chatterton knew him no more, but became a regular attendant at Temple where his friend of Noachian fame held forth. Therein he had other purposes than to be instructed concerning the voyage of the ark. The vicar of Temple had books, and he had more, an influence strong enough to get the boy past the jealously guarded gates of the Bristol Library, or that is to say, into Paradise. This being presently accomplished, it may be supposed that his interest in a very uninspiring acquaintance came to an end. Yet not altogether so; he subsequently satirized the vicar in some cutting verses, and then, with characteristic good-heartedness, regretted them and hoped the vicar did not take the raillery to heart. "When the fit is on me," he said, "I spare neither friend nor foe," and thus embalmed the name of one that would not otherwise linger in the human memory. In one respect, Alexander Catcott had more wit than his brother: he knew when he was laughed at, and it appears that to forgive an injury he was not so ready as became a preacher of the gospel.

Once inside of Bristol Library, the boy ranged as far as his time would permit. Curious evidences of his labors still exist there. One of the treasures of that library is an old black letter Latin Dictionary, called "Promptorum Puerorum," printed at Strasburg, part of it in 1484 and part in 1496. On some of the pages of this book some one that wrote much like Chatterton has been hard at work, making studies and copies of the ancient characters. On one page appears a date, "September, 1763," in the old letters, and elsewhere another date, "4th day July, 1463," four times repeated, each time slightly enlarged and changed. On the same page is "Liber D.B. ex domo," done in the old character, "D. B." being the initials over which Chatterton often wrote. On the margin of this page he has worked out an alphabet, capitals and lower case, and on other pages are traces of his busy pen, including some practise at the name "Catcott," all in imitation of the black-letter in which the book is printed. Chatterton wrote in a very clean, clear, copper-plate hand, not hard to recognize. I am certain that all these experiments in the old dictionary are his.

He was now far advanced in the Rowley poems and, knowing so well the English poetry of his own and other times, it was impossible that he should not perceive the art worth of his work. He determined to bring some of it to the test of such criticism as the time afforded. James Dodsley of Pall Mall, of a family whose memory is green for its service to good literature, was then the most famous publisher and bookseller in England. He was of much wealth, some liberality of taste, rather unusual repute for scholarly inclinings and of solitary and eccentric habits. His business training had doubtless been stern in the ways of convention. He must have been somewhat astonished, therefore, at two letters that he received about this time from an unknown correspondent in Bristol. The first read as follows:

BRISTOL, December 21, 1768.

SIR, — I take this method to acquaint you that I can procure copys of several Ancient Poems: and an interlude, perhaps the oldest dramatic piece extant; wrote by one Rowley, a priest in

Bristol, who lived in the reigns of Henry VIth and Edward IVth. If these pieces will be of service to you, at your command copys will be sent to you by,

Y^r most obedient serv^t,

D. B.

Please to direct for D. B., to be left with Mr. Thos. Chatterton, Redcliffe Hill, Bristol.

To this polite overture Dodsley returned no answer. Chatterton, not discouraged, renewed the attack in a second letter, February 15, 1769. There were reasons why of all publishers he should fix upon Dodsley as the man likeliest to suit his purposes, for Dodsley was believed in those days to have abnormal knowledge of and interest in ancient literature. But in the interim the boy must have turned over in his mind the possible reasons why his first communication had been neglected. It seemed to him likely that the trouble lay in the undue brevity, initialed signature, and lack of detail in his letter. So in his next communication he remedied these defects in artless fashion and produced an epistle calculated to astonish any recipient. He wrote as follows:

Sir, — Having intelligence that the Tragedy of Aella was in being, after a long and laborious search, I was so happy as to attain a sight of it. Struck with the beauties of it, I endeavoured to obtain a copy of it to send to you; but the present possessor absolutely denies to give me one, unless I give him a Guinea for a consideration. As I am unable to procure such a sum, I made search for another copy, but unsuccessfully. Unwilling such a beauteous Piece should be lost, I have made bold to apply to you; several Gentlemen of learning, who have seen it, join with me in praising it. I am far from having any mercenary views for myself in this affair, and, was I able, would print it at my own risque. It is a perfect Tragedy; the plot clear, the language spirited, and the Songs (interspersed in it) are flowing, poetical and elegantly simple; the similes judiciously applied, and though wrote in the reign of Henry VI, not inferior to many of the present age. If I can procure a copy, with or without the gratification, it shall immediately be sent to you. The motive that actuates me to do this is, to convince the world that the Monks (of whom some have so despicable an opinion) were not such blockheads as generally thought, and that good poetry might be wrote in the dark days of superstition, as well as in these more enlightened ages. An immediate answer will oblige. I shall not receive your favour as for myself but as your agent.

I am, Sir, your most obedient servant,

THOMAS CHATTERTON.

P. S. — My reason for concealing my name was lest my master (who is now out of town) should see my letters, and think I neglected his business. Direct for me on Redcliffe Hill.

With this he sent an extract from the tragedy. At a bald proposition to forward a guinea to a youth of whom he had no knowledge Dodsley might well be startled. Naturally he did not respond with the guinea, and if he acknowledged the receipt of the letter the boy kept the answer to himself. The prim and precise bookseller of Pall Mall was not likely to be impressed favorably with a youth that was avowedly misusing his master's time, and the "Tragedy of Aella" was not given to the world through the famous Dodsley.

And yet he had never in his career published anything greater, and if the extract he received made any just representation of the piece it is incomprehensible how he failed to see that whether Rowley were true or false here was a most extraordinary piece of work. For the "Tragedy of Aella" is not only the greatest of all the Rowley poems, but a work that purporting to be of any age from any hand would be recognized now as the certain product of genius. In that age it shines like a diamond in an ash-heap. Nothing comparable with it had been written since Milton; nothing equal to it came afterward until Shelley.

It has long been the custom to refer to the works of Chatterton as wonderful for a boy. In truth, mostly they would be wonderful for a man. Even now when the purely artistic view of poetry (of which he was the first exponent) has so many years dominated and developed our verse and carried it along the undreamed-of ways to heights equal with its sister arts, it is impossible to read with attention the "Tragedy of Aella" without being moved to admiration of its sheer art and exquisite workmanship.

This is the story: Aella is the Saxon lord of the Castle of Bristol, a great warrior and leader. He has taken to wife Birtha, young, high-born, and beautiful. On their wedding-night, when with song and chorus the minstrels are entertaining the banqueters at the wedding feast, news comes that the Dacians (or Danes) have landed and are ravaging the coast. Aella, in spite of his bride's entreaties, seizes his arms and rushes away to the war. In a great battle at Watchet he meets and routs the Danish army, and having meantime burned the Danish fleet he has the invaders at his mercy.

His lieutenant, Celmonde, has long been secretly in love with Birtha. With gloomy and Iago-like malice he has watched the wedding festivities, and from the war he thinks to win either the woman he loves or revenge for his disappointment. He is brave enough, but bad. At once after the battle of Watchet he takes horse and rides at great speed to Bristol. In the middle of the night he reaches the castle, and tells Birtha that Aella, sorely wounded, has sent for her. In a frenzy of fear she runs from the castle without delaying to tell her serving woman. Celmonde is to guide her to the spot where Aella lies. In the dark woods he seizes her and declares his passion. She struggles from him and screams for help. A band of fugitive Danes with their leader, Hurra, hear her. Celmonde fights desperately against overwhelming odds and slays many, but is slain by Hurra. The Danes learn that they have in hand the wife of the man that defeated them, but magnanimously protect her and undertake to lead her to Aella's camp.

But in the meantime Aella has come home in triumph to share with his bride the news and glory of the great victory. He finds that Birtha has gone away with a knight and none knows whither. Convinced that she has proved false he stabs himself. As he lies on his bed Birtha comes in. They are reconciled, but Aella dies of his wound, and Birtha, flinging herself upon his body, dies of grief.

After the strength and interest of the story and the dramatic power of its unfolding, the first impression this play makes on us is of the infinite skill of its handling within the narrow limits of a difficult stanza. This is the Rowleyan ten-line stanza used elsewhere, but not as here with masterly strength and art in terse, rapid, and at times impassioned dialogue. I will give a specimen of this peculiar achievement. Aella has reached his door after his return from the battle of Watchet. Egwina, Birtha's tiring woman, meets him.

Egwina. Oh Aella!
Aella.   Ah! that semmlykeene [1] to mee
Speeketh a legendary tale of woe.
Eg. Birtha is —
Ael.   Whatt ? where ? how ? saie, whatte of shee ?

[1] Appearance.

Eg. Gone —

Ael.   Gone! ye goddes!

Eg.   Alas! ytte ys toe true.

Yee seynctes, hee dies awaie wythe myckle woe!

Aella! what? Aella! oh! hee lyves agen!

Ael. Cal mee notte Aella; I am hymme ne moe.

Where ys shee gon awaie? Ah! Speake! how? when?

Eg. I will.

Ael. Caparyson a score of stedes; flie, flie!

Where ys shee? Swythynne [1] speeke, or instante thou shalt die.

These lines constitute one Rowleyan stanza. The play bears title as follows:

Aella,

A Tragycal Enterlude,

or Discoorseynge Tragedie,

Wrotenn bie

Thomas Rowleie;

Plaiedd before

Mastre Canynge,

Atte hys howse nempte the Rodde Lodge;

Alsoe before the Duke of Norfolck,

Johan Howard.

In all England there was not at that time enough scholarship to know that in the reign of Edward IV the only theatrical performances were religious Mystery or Miracle plays done by monks in the churches, and that such a thing as a secular play was unknown until almost a century later. Hun-

[1] Quickly.

dreds of men from the universities knew the histories of the Greek and Roman dramas and could discourse learnedly about Greek prosody, and not one knew the drama of his own country or the history of his country's language.

There are thirteen different measures in "Aella," all (except the blank verse and the quatrain) being innovations in our metrical systems.   First come, in different measures, two letters to Canynge purporting to have been written by Rowley and signed with his name.   The second hints at the theory, held by Chatterton, of poetry as an art; that is, of art poetry as distinguished from mere verse.   "Verse may be good," he says, "but poetry wants more, a boundless subject and a worthy song of it"; and he rails at the scholars that hold to a literal view of everything and have no idealism.   "Instead of mounting on a winged horse," he goes on, having an eye to the rule-and-compass poetasters of his own day, "You on a cart-horse drive in doleful course."

> [1]Canynge and I from common course dissent,
>   We ride the steed, but give to him the rein,
> Nor will between crazed moldering books be pent,
>   But soar on high, amid the sunbeams' sheen.

"An Entroductionne" of two stanzas follows, and then the "Personnes Represented":

[1] Modernized.

Aella,   bie Thomas Rowleie, Preeste, the Aucthoure.
Celmonde,   John Iscamm, Preeste.
Hurra,   Syrr Thybbotte Gorges, Knyghte.
Birtha,   Mastre Edwarde Canynge.
  Odherr Parties bie Knyghtes, Mynstrelles, *&c.*

The play begins with a brief soliloquy by Celmonde
in which he resents his fate that he must see the
woman he has loved become the wife of another, and
then follow the wedding festivities, varied with songs
that are among the ablest examples of Chatterton's art.
Few English poets have had equal power over melodi-
ous speech and few have had so much prescience
about the subtle co-relations between music and
poetry.   Indeed, the purely musical phase of modern
English poetry may be said to have begun with him.
    The first of the songs in "Aella" is a simple
pastoral dialogue between a country maiden and her
swain, but the lilt of it is extraordinary, the effect
being managed to some degree through the use of
the trochaic measure, the musical possibilities of
which Chatterton was the first to discover.

Tourne thee to thie Shepsterr swayne ;
Bryghte sonne has ne droncke the dewe
From the floures of yellowe hue;
Tourne thee, Alyce, backe agayne.

No, bestoikerre, I wylle go,
Softlie tryppynge o'ere the mees,
Lyche the sylver-footed doe,
Seekeynge shelterr yn grene trees.

See the moss-growne daisey'd banke,
Pereynge ynne the streme belowe;
Here we'lle sytte, yn dewie danke;
Tourne thee, Alyce, do notte goe.

It is chiefly the spelling that is a bar to the easy reading and swift appreciation of Chatterton. To modernize these stanzas requires scarcely an effort. If we know that "bestoikerre" means deceiver and "mees" means meadows, there is not a line in it that cannot be understood by a child.

Aella praises the song, but asks for one that "marriage blessings tells."

"In marriage, blessings are but few, I trowe," comments the embittered Celmonde in a cynical aside. The minstrels sing:

Fyrste Mynstrelle

The boddynge flourettes bloshes atte the lyghte,
The mees be sprenged wyth the yellowe hue;
Ynn daiseyd mantels ys the mountayne dyghte;
The nesh yonge coweslepe bendethe wyth the dewe;
The trees enlefed, yntoe Heavenne straughte,
Whenn gentle wyndes doe blowe, to whestlyng dynne ys broughte.

The evenynge commes, and brynges the dewe alonge;
The roddie welkynne sheeneth to the eyne;
Arounde the alestake Mynstrelles synge the songe;
Yonge ivie rounde the doore poste do entwyne;
I laie mee onn the grasse; yette, to mie wylle,
Albeytte alle ys fayre, there lacketh somethynge stylle.

Second Mynstrelle

So Adam thoughtenne, whann, ynn Paradyse,
All Heavenn and Erthe dyd hommage to hys mynde;
Ynn Womman alleyne mannes pleasaunce lyes;
As instrumentes of joie were made the kynde.
Go, take a wyfe untoe thie armes, and see
Wynter, and brownie hylles, wyll have a charme for thee.

Thyrde Mynstrelle

Whanne Autumpne blake and sonne-brente doe appere,
Wyth hys goulde honde guylteynge the falleynge lefe,
Bryngeynge oppe Wynterr to folfylle the yere
Beerynge uponne hys backe the riped shefe;
Whan al the hyls wythe woddie sede ys whyte;
Whanne levynne-fyres and lemes do mete from far the syghte;

Whann the fayre apple, rudde as even skie,
Do bende the tree unto the fructyle grounde;
When joicie peres, and berries of blacke die,
Doe daunce yn ayre, and call the eyne arounde;
Thann, bee the even foule, or even fayre,
Meethynckes mie hartys joie ys steynced with somme care.

Seconde Mynstrelle

Angelles bee wrogte to bee of neidher kynde;
Angelles alleyne fromme chafe desyre bee free:
Dheere ys a somwhatte evere yn the mynde,
Yatte, wythout wommanne, cannot stylled bee;
Ne seyncte yn celles, botte, havynge blodde and tere,
Do fynde the spryte to joie on syghte of wommanne fayre

Wommen bee made, notte for hemselves botte manne,
Bone of hys bone, and chyld of hys desire;
Fromme an ynutylle membere fyrste beganne,

Ywroghte with moche of water, lyttele fyre;
Therefore theie seke the fyre of love, to hete
The milkyness of kynde, and make hemselves complete.

Albeytte, wythout wommen, menne were pheeres
To salvage kynde, and wulde botte lyve to slea,
Botte wommenne efte the spryghte of peace so cheres,
Tochelod yn Angel joie heie Angeles bee;
Go, take thee swythyn to thie bedde a wyfe,
Bee bante or blessed hie yn proovynge marryage lyfe.

It may seem superfluous to attempt any modern version of this beautiful poem, since with slight changes in its spelling most of the words are familiar in our every-day speech; but to show how this is and to ease the reading I give some of the most significant stanzas a garb more familiar if less harmonious:

When Autumn bleak and sunburnt doth appear,
With his gold hand gilding the falling leaf,
Bringing up Winter to fulfil the year,
Bearing upon his back the ripened sheaf,
When all the hills with woolly seed are white,
When lightning-fires and gleams do meet from far the sight;

When the fair apples, red as evening sky,
Down bend the tree unto the fruitful ground,
When juicy pears and berries of black dye
Do dance in air, and call the eyes around;
Then, be the evening foul or be it fair,
Methinks my heart's delight is marred with some dark care.

And the last stanza:

> Albeit, without woman, men were peers
> To savage kind, and would but live to slay;
> But woman that the soul of peace so cheers,
> Wrapped in angelic joy wings her high way;
> Go, take thee quickly to thy bed a wife,
> Be cursed or highly blessed in proving married life.

This song of the seasons is followed by "Anodher Mynstrelles Songe," attributed to Syr Thybbot Gorges. It has the swinging beat and exquisite musical adjustment that characterize all the Rowley lyrics. For the meter there are in a way two English precedents, something like it though crudely wrought, one to be found in that curious and mysterious fourteenth century exotic, "The Coke's Tale of Gamelyn," once ascribed to Chaucer; the other in the old English ballad, "The Blind Beggar's Daughter of Bednall Green." But while these two unknown poets made some use of the amphibrach foot as here, Chatterton was the first of modern singers to perceive the musical potentialities of occasional syncopation, and to weave it into a melody, here extremely blithesome and taking:

> As Elynour bie the green lesselle [1] was syttynge,
> As from the sones hete she harried, [2]
> She sayde, as herr whytte hondes whyte hosen was knyttynge,
> What pleasure ytt ys to be married!

---

[1] lesselle — lattice.   [2] harried — hurried.

Mie husbande, Lorde Thomas, a forrester boulde,
   As ever clove pynne,[1] or the baskette,
Does no cherysauncys[2] from Elynour houlde,
   I have ytte as soone as I aske ytte.

Whann I lyved wyth my fadre yn merrie Clowd-dell,
   Tho' twas at my liefe[3] to mynde spynnynge,
I stylle wanted somethynge, botte whatte ne coulde telle,
   Mie lorde fadres barbde[4] haulle han ne wynnynge.[5]

Eche mornynge I ryse, doe I sette mie maydennes,
   Somme to spynn, somme to curdell, somme bleachynge,
Gyff[6] any new entered doe aske for mie aidens,[7]
   Thann swythynne[8] you fynde mee a teachynge.

Lorde Walterre, mie fadre, he loved me welle,
   And nothynge unto mee was nedeynge,
Botte schulde I agen goe to merrie Cloud-dell
   In sothen[9] twoulde bee wythoute redeynge.[10]

Shee sayde, and lorde Thomas came over the lea,
   As hee the fatte derkynnes[11] was chacynge,
Shee putte uppe her knyttynge, and to hym wente shee;
   So wee leave hem bothe kyndelie embracynge.

Here and there in the tragedy are stanzas of
extraordinary beauty and strength. For instance,

---

[1] Clove pin or the basket refers to targets at rustic archery matches.

[2] cherisauncys — comforts.   [3] liefe — at my choice.

[4] barbde haulle — hall hung with armor.

[5] Wynnynge — could not be won there.

[6] Gyff — If.   [7] Aidens — Help.

[8] Swythynne — Quickly.   [9] Sothen — faith.

[10] Redeynge — redeing. The line means "In faith it would be without good
counsel, ill-advised."   [11] Derkynnes — deer.

in a soliloquy of Celmonde's just after Aella has gone forth to meet the Danes:

> Hope, holy sister, sweeping through the skies,
> In crown of gold, and robe of lily white
> That broadly on the gentle breezes flies,
> Meeting from distance the enraptured sight,
> Although thou often takest thy high flight
> Wrapped in a mist and with thy sweet eyes blind,
> Now comest thou to me with starry light;
> Unto thy vest red sunbeams thou dost bind;
> The Summer-tide, the month of May, appear
> With cunning skill upon thy wide robe painted clear.[1]

Aella delivers a tremendous battle speech before his army, a speech that makes one think of Shakespeare's Henry before the battle of Agincourt, really a great speech. I quote the end of it:

> I say no more; your souls the rest will say,
> Your souls will show that Bristol is their place;
> To honor's house I need not mark the way,
> In your own hearts ye may the foot-path trace.
> 'Tween fate and us there is but little space;
> The time is now to prove yourselves. Be men!
> Draw forth the burnished bill with festive grace!
> Rouse, like a wolf when rousing from his den!
> Thus I pluck forth my weapon! Go, thou sheath!
> I'll put it not in place till it is sick with death!

[1] This and other selections following I have modernized.

Soldiers. On, Aella, on! We long for bloody fray,
We long to hear the raven sing in vain.
On, Aella on! We surely gain the day
When thou dost lead us to the deadly plain!

Celmonde tells of the battle, of the prowess of Aella and the triumphing Saxon arms, and in his story is this passage:

Bright sun had in his ruddy robes been dight;
From the red East he flitted with his train;
The hours drew aside the veil of night,
Her sable tapestry was rent in twain.
The dancing streaks bedecked the heavens wide plain,
And on the dew did smile with shimmering eye.

Celmonde is something like Franz Moor; just before he starts on his despicable errand he has a soliloquy that reasons of good and evil much after the manner of Schiller's villain, in which he concludes that

" — eternal fame — it is but air
Bred in the phantasy and only living there."

And again:

Albeit everything in life conspire
To tell me of the fault I now should do,
Yet would I recklessly assuage my fire,
And the same means, as I shall now, pursue.
The qualities I from my parents drew
Were blood and murder, mastery and war;
These I will hold to now, and heed no moe
A wound in honor than a body-scar.

The song that is sung before Birtha mourning for the absent Aella, though no doubt suggested by Ophelia's song in Hamlet,

His beard was white as snow, *etc.*

has, nevertheless, lyrical and other qualities that transcend in interest any considerations of possible plagiarism. Chatterton had the soul of a musician and such a sense of sound values as no English poet before him had ever displayed. In this song, for instance, whoever has interest in the development of our modern system of poetry may note the appearance of the designed use of the rest towards a certain musical effect as in Swinburne and others in these times. The tempo here is intended to be slow and stately, as befits the mournful theme, and it is secured by the one means of the interposed rest at regular intervals. I will give two stanzas and then show the musical theory they are built upon.

> O! synge untoe mie roundelaie,
> O! droppe the brynie teare wythe mee,
> Daunce ne moe atte hallie daie,
> Lycke a reynynge ryver bee;
>> Mie love ys dedde,
>> Gon to hys death-bedde,
>> Al under the wyllowe tree.

> See! the whyte moone sheenes onne hie;
> Whyterre ys mie true loves shroude;

Whyterre yanne the mornynge skie,
Whyterre yanne the evenynge cloude;
    Mie love ys dedde,
    Gon to hys deathe-bedde,
    Al under the wyllowe tree.

This has the following musical scheme:

O! sing un - to my round - e - lay,

O! drop the brin - y tear with me,

Dance no more on hol - i - day,

Like a run - ning riv - er be;

My love is dead,

gone to his death - bed

All un - der the will - low tree.

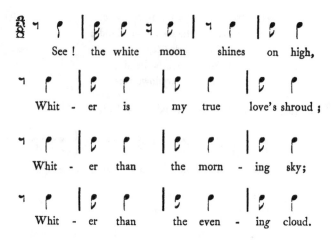

See! the white moon shines on high,
Whit - er is my true love's shroud;
Whit - er than the morn - ing sky;
Whit - er than the even - ing cloud.

The device of the rest at the beginning of the line creates the impression of solemn utterance and slow tempo, and materially influences the total effect. The song is one of the most melancholy in the language and one of the sweetest of sound. To manage the music of words to a melody so simple and still so moving is the gift of the gods. Few of our race have had it.

> Comme, wythe acorne-coppe and thorne,
> Drayne mie hartys blodde awaie;
> Lyfe and all yttes goode I scorne,
> Daunce bie nete, or feaste by daie.
>   Mie love ys dedde,
>   Gon to hys death-bedde,
>   Al under the wyllowe tree.

Waterre wytches, crownede wythe reytes,
Bere mee to yer leathalle tyde.
I die! I comme! mie true love waytes.
Thos the damselle spake and dyed.

Some other instances of the poet's marvelous skill
may be given from this poem:

[1] The world is dark with night, the winds are still;
Faintly the moon her pallid light makes gleam;
The risen sprites the silent churchyard fill,
With elfin fairies joining in the dream;
The forest shineth with the silver leme.

.   .   .   .

I have a mind winged with the lightning's plume.

.   .   .   .

[1] This darkness doth affray my woman's breast;
How sable is the spreading sky arrayed!
Happy the cottager who lives to rest
Nor is at Night's all-daunting hue dismayed.
The stars do scantily the sable braid,
Wide are the silver gleams of comfort wove.
Speak, Celmonde, doth it make thee not afraid?

.   .   .   .

The mornynge 'gyns alonge the easte to sheene;
Darklinge the lyghte doe onne the waters plaie;
The feynte rodde leme slowe creepeth oere the greene,
Toe chase the merkyness of nyghte awaie;
Swifte flie the howers thatte wylle brynge oute the daie;
The softe dewe falleth onne the greeynge grasse;
The shepster mayden, dyghtynge her arraie,
Scante sees her vysage yn the wavie glasse.

[1] Modernized.

Lest so fine a stanza should be lost for a few tricks of spelling I give it also in modern dress:

> The morn begins along the east to shine,
> Darkling the light doth on the waters play,
> The faint red gleam slow creepeth o'er the green
> To chase the murkiness of night away;
> Swift fly the hours that will bring out the day;
> The soft dew falleth on the growing grass;
> The shepherd-maiden, dighting her array,
> Scarce sees her image in the wavy glass.

A certain power of condensed and pithy expression is apparent throughout this remarkable play. The characters habitually say no more than they ought to say and speak pointedly. The temptation to spin out the last scene with death-bed speeches would have been irresistible except to an artist. There is a kind of eloquent brevity about the scene as Chatterton handles it, reminding one of the Greek tragedies. Mr. Swinburne has hardly done better in such a notable ending as that of "Rosamund." When Birtha appears and in wonderfully few lines the situation is made clear, this ensues:

> *Aella.* Oh! I die contente. (Dieth)
> *Birtha.* Oh! ys mie Aella dedde?
> Oh! I wylle make hys grave mie vyrgyn spousal bedde.
>   (Birtha feyncteth.)

Dodsley did not accept "Aella," the tragedy reposed in the possession of Catcott, and the world had no knowledge of it until after the great strange mind that wrought it had left these shifting scenes.

With another brief correspondence we have more to do. After the failure with Dodsley, whatever might have been the cause of it, Chatterton was more than ever determined to give Rowley to the world, and thereupon faced a problem that has puzzled and sometimes overwhelmed many an older writer. He must find a medium; and for a boy fifteen years old, apprentice to an obscure lawyer in a provincial town, the task was of the hardest. In the Rowley romance the priest-poet and hero was befriended and helped by a wealthy, judicious patron, the friend of art and artists. Nothing could be more natural than for the reincarnated Rowley (if I may use that term) to seek a rich man of taste, intelligence, and literary discernment that might be the reincarnated Canynge. One such there was in England by chance and not by merit raised to that eminence. Horace Walpole, Earl of Orford, among his many posings found time to pose as a patron of literature. He had a private press at Strawberry Hill, he maintained a friendship with Gray of the Elegy and with other literary men of the day, and as a dilettante wrote some things himself. He was rich, eminent, and influential. Moreover there was a particular reason why Chatterton should be attracted to him, for Walpole had not long before fabricated his Otranto disguise and gone forth in it to the public, and he might reasonably, therefore, be thought to have a sympathetic feeling for the like masqueraders. Chatterton determined to appeal to Horace Walpole.

The strange fact about the correspondence that followed is that Barrett, the strait-laced surgeon, seems to have known all about Chatterton's share in it and to have, in a measure at least, directed his young friend's course. Certainly the surgeon drafted some of the letters and he could hardly have drafted them without knowing the whole history of the affair. Here, as before, then, we come upon this silent, stealthy figure as the cloaked director of the visible moves. Perhaps Barrett was the real knave of the piece; perhaps he suggested Walpole and knew all along the character of the pretended manuscripts; who shall say? Walpole's "Anecdotes of Painting" was then a highly esteemed fruitage of the Strawberry Hill garden and offered an easy avenue of approach to that home of the muses. Consequently Chatterton addressed him thus:

SIR, — Being versed a little in antiquitys, I have met with several curious manuscripts, among which the following may be of service to you, in any future edition of your truly entertaining "Anecdotes of Painting." In correcting the mistakes (if any) in the notes you will greatly oblige

Your most humble servant,

THOMAS CHATTERTON.

BRISTOL, March 25th, Corn Street.

The manuscript accompanying purported to be a transcription of one entitled "The Ryse of Peyncteyne yn Englande, wroten by T. Rowleie, 1469, for Mastre Canynge." The notes cunningly introduced the whole Rowley romance and contained a bait for the owner of the Strawberry Hill press, for they said that whoever might publish the Rowley poems would lay the Englishman, the antiquary, and the poet under an eternal obligation.

It was this boy's fate all his life to deal with the fraudulent or the foolish or with those that were both. If Walpole had really possessed a modicum of the literary acumen to which he pretended, or if he had been a man of any worth, there would be a different story to tell of Thomas Chatterton. At first the author of Otranto was vastly taken with the discovery of Rowley. He replied to Chatterton in an effusive letter, regarded the "Ryse of Peyncteyne" as a wonderful addition to his store of knowledge, and intimated a willingness to print the Rowley poems.

Thus encouraged, Chatterton wrote again, revealing his situation as a poor boy, the son of a widow, the apprentice of an attorney, but with an ambition for a literary career. All that he said we shall never know, Walpole having, for reasons of his own, destroyed a part of his letter, but it is certain that he spoke quite frankly of the facts in his case; Walpole has admitted as much. He enclosed another prose manuscript and a specimen of Rowley's poetry, being the Ode to War already quoted from "The Battle of Hastings." Walpole had not counted on dealing with penniless sons of obscure widows; the boy's candor utterly changed his attitude. He showed the manuscripts to Gray of the Elegy and to Gray's friend Mason. They said the work was not of the fifteenth century; whereupon Walpole favored Chatterton with a letter of cold advice, declining to be of any assistance to him and telling him with brutal irony to labor hard at being a scrivener and when he had amassed a fortune at that trade he might turn his attention to literary studies.

But he kept the manuscripts, that is the strange thing; he kept the manuscripts. What for only heaven knows; perhaps to copy and use them, a dastardly act, of which, by his own confession, he was quite capable. Chatterton wrote thrice, the last two letters being courteous but firm demands, for the return of his property. Walpole afterward declared that he was preparing to go to Paris when these epistles arrived and, doubtless, in the stress and confusion of that momentous and necessary work, the intrusive protests of a mere apprentice of the lower orders were overlooked. The last of the letters was dated July 24, and in Horace Walpole's opinion it was "singularly impertinent," being addressed by a very common person to one of the nobility. It read:

SIR, — I cannot reconcile your behaviour to me with the notions I once entertained of you. I think myself injured, Sir: and did not you know of my circumstances you would not dare to treat me thus. I have sent twice for a copy of the MS. — no answer from you. An explanation or excuse for your silence would oblige,
THOMAS CHATTERTON.

Walpole said afterward that on the receipt of this revolutionary and insulting communication he took his pen in hand and began a letter of admonition and expostulation, but probably concluding that the young ruffian was beyond hope and incorrigible, he flung the letter he had begun into the fire, and snapping up Chatterton's manuscripts and letters he returned them without a word. In later years, when he came to deny that he had ever received certain of these letters, the fact that he did not have them was of use to him. In the minds of some persons it helped to relieve the figure he cut, which was really one of the sorriest in literary history. The boy was perfectly right in his conclusion that if Walpole had not known of the condition of his correspondent he would not have dared to use him so. Whatever might have been the verdict of Gray and Mason, there could be no excuse for returning the manuscripts without an acknowledgment, and no possible palliation for retaining them so long. Even

Coleridge when he had fallen from grace and turned reactionary gagged at this. But, on the whole, the earl of Orford has escaped lightly; on the whole, the abundant literature of denunciation that the Chatterton story has called forth seems to have been unevenly distributed, and one would be pleased to record that a part of the wrath that fell upon the memory of the young apprentice had been reserved for the knavish nobleman.

The fall of his hopes went nigh for the moment to crush the boy. He had counted so much upon the modern Canynge as his friendly helper in the task he had set for himself and there had been so much reason for his faith! This was the one man of the age that held such a position, or seemed to hold it, as the builder of St. Mary Redcliffe had held; the man of taste and wealth, the friend of poets, the man that had printed at his own expense "The Elegy in a Country Churchyard," the poem that Chatterton felt Rowley could far surpass. And this man would not see, this man thought the obvious and trite reflections of Gray were better than the divine art that he could show him! And the cold insult he had endured — that was only because he was poor and obscure, that was a gratuitous reminder that he was far below the caste to which the noblemen of the realm belonged, that he was only a boy of the lower classes and must take what treatment his betters might please to give him, that he must not dream of addressing them. The iron entered his soul as he thought of it. The world was against him, the channels to recognition and expression were solely possessed by the fortunate; henceforth, a solitary and friendless waif, he was flung in a desperate struggle against those invincible barriers.

The villainy you teach me I will execute and it shall go hard but I will better the instruction.

He had been flogged for reading and dreaming, flogged for writing poetry, upbraided by his master for wasting his time in study, cajoled and mistreated by the scheming Barrett and the foolish Catcott, neglected by every one that should have taken an intelligent interest in him, enslaved to a drudging occupation, grossly and wantonly insulted by the man that was supposed to be the criterion of the literary taste of his day, reminded that he was not of the class that might be allowed to succeed, thrust back among the unthinking hinds to whose lowly ways he properly belonged, made in one flash to see how great a gulf separated him from the elect, scorned for his beautiful work that his age would have none of, defeated on every hand. And still the indomitable spirit burned high within him, still exalted by a sense of his calling, the insuperable knowledge of his gift, and the fervor for expression, he toiled on alone. But from this time he had less regard than ever for the means by which he should wring from the hard world the recognition that merely because he was young and poor that world had denied to him.

The restless spirit of this strange being had, meantime, found another and wholly different channel for its activities. I have said something of his intense interest in the political affairs of his day. In these all the part of his nature that was not dreamer and artist was now deeply engrossed. The time was ripe for one of his faith. The England of his day was passing through one of those convulsive struggles between surviving feudalism and young democracy from which have come, by slow degrees, the present emancipated race. It was, in fact, one of the dying tremors of absolutism, though nobody of that day so viewed it. For a few years the foolish George III had been on the throne doing many foolish things, and now with characteristic folly and obstinacy he was standing out for the medieval right of the monarch to choose his own ministers, no matter how distasteful they might be to the nation. Past this blockade, in a way not without precedent in human affairs, progress was unwittingly furthered by an obtuse prejudice as much as by the agitation carried on by the popular leaders. The minister most detested happened to be a Scot, and the cardinal principles of the Englishman of that day were to fear God and hate the Scotch. We should be profoundly thankful that the Scotch had traits offensive to the English mind; otherwise England might to-day have a constitution like Germany's. The Scotchman for whom the foolish king stood fast was the Earl of Bute, a well-enough meaning man, no doubt, but deficient in tact and unluckily the target of much abuse because he was a favorite with that acrid and unpopular person, the king's mother. Bute was prime minister, a great many things went awry, as things will go, more or less; the premier was accused, on plausible grounds, of incompetency, and a hot agitation began to induce the king to remove him. Inevitably the discussion verged upon other delicate points concerning ruler and ruled, the spirit of revolt that presently flamed out in the American and French revolutions was tugging at the minds of men, and soon there arose a leader capable of directing the new movement and making himself its idol.

This was the misunderstood John Wilkes. For almost a century and a half English writers have been pleased to denounce this man as a demagogue, but in the clearer perspective of time and the better lights we have on such things we need not be too sure of his demagogy. With all its faults, many things in the life of John Wilkes seem eminently respectable. He cheerfully endured imprisonment and risked far worse for the sake of a good cause. Almost everything he stood for has had the infrangible endorsement of posterity and the honor of a place in the British constitution. No one can now doubt that in preventing him from taking his seat because he had criticized the king, the House of Commons was absolutely in the wrong, absolutely guilty of a tyrannical and reactionary excess. That Wilkes was bitterly hated by the court party and that the court interest then, as always, had the loudest voice and wrote (and distorted) the most history need not concern us. The king and the monarchial interest generally were engaged in supporting and enforcing a purely feudal institution. They were bravely opposed by one man. He may not have been very nice about some things; liberty habitually chooses the uncouth and the extravagant to wield her weapons; conventional men and those that travel on the main trodden highways of propriety seldom feel much of her fire. Moreover, in all history invariably the man that has stood for the common people has been pictured by the powers of reaction as a depraved person; he must be depraved or he would not oppose the interests of those divinely appointed to be fortunate and to possess the earth. Whatever defects of character John Wilkes may have had, he did stand for democracy, he did battle with hand and brain and voice against tyranny and the backward step, he did effect an advance, and for these tremendous services the judicious can afford to overlook the worst that has been charged against him.

Into the fight then waging for democracy this boy threw himself with all the ardor of his soul. It was a course that had naturally the strongest attractions for him; the boy that gave his last pennies to the poor of Bristol could not feel otherwise. Besides, among his convictions were a profound contempt for convention and a prophetic sense of the future of mankind. The great poets that have made the paths whereon our poetry has traveled have been of this stamp: Marlowe, Milton the Republican, Shelley, Swinburne; the innovators have been the radicals, the men impatient of feudalism, indignant against the trammels of caste and established conditions, rebels and often outcasts. That a man should feel beauty enough to be a great poet he must feel deeply also for men. Always the poets have been mighty on the side of democracy if they have been great enough to endure; as do but think of Dante, Massinger, Lessing, even Schiller, and above all the supreme light of Victor Hugo, besides the great group we have already spoken of. Who knows but it was this that cost Surrey his head? And for all his later backsliding Coleridge was of the valiant brood so long as opium had left his wits clear. In our own day we have seen poets become socialists like Morris, and a whole brood of American singers; fervent champions of the broadest democracy like Whitman; fiery and uncontrollable revolutionists like Swinburne; friends of the oppressed and the suffering like William Watson. He was of this angelic brotherhood, he too, this boy; he was for democracy, and the keen sword of his satire was out against king, prime-minister, and all surviving oppression.

We accept these things now as a matter of course, but consider for a moment the strength of character and the sincerity of purpose necessary for such a choice at such a time. For the champions of reaction were pensions and preferments, soft places and the favor of the court and of the powerful in a day when the ablest writer could hardly expect without aid to earn a bare subsistence. For those that wrote on the patriotic side was nothing but starvation pittances and the danger of prosecution. To an ambitious young man just beginning his career as a writer, one service offered an easy ascent to comfort and fame and the other held forth poverty and obscurity. That Chatterton never hesitated in the face of such temptations is a fact clearly entitling him to our utmost respect; although here, as in so many other instances, the recognition due him has always been denied.

There was ample occasion for the enlisting of any

democrat. Wilkes, a member of Parliament, had been editor of a weekly newspaper called the *North Briton*. In this he ventured in 1763 to print some criticism of a speech of the king's. He was arrested but pleaded his Parliamentary privileges, and after some days in the Tower was released. He thereupon reprinted the issue of the *North Briton* that had criticized the King, and the House of Commons expelled him and passed a special act to provide for his prosecution. Wilkes was then on the Continent. He was prosecuted for his attack on the King, and also for printing the "Essay on Woman,"[1] found guilty, and, not appearing for sentence, was outlawed. He returned to England, stood for Middlesex, was triumphantly elected, and over the vital issue thus created the conservative, land-owning, king-worshiping Commons and the progressive element among the people were locked in a memorable struggle that lasted for years. The House refused to admit Wilkes and declared his seat vacant. He had in the meantime surrendered himself to the process of the law, had been fined £1000, sentenced to twenty-two months imprisonment, and shut up in jail. Middlesex promptly re-elected him; the Commons refused to admit him and again declared his seat vacant.

[1] It has often been represented that Wilkes was the author of this obscene poem. The real author was Thomas Potter, son of the Archbishop of Canterbury. But thirteen copies of it were printed on Wilkes's press, and this fact was seized as a pretext for prosecuting Wilkes.

By this time people were in a white heat elsewhere as well as in London. Twice again Middlesex elected the man of its choice; twice again the Commons rejected him. But on the last occasion the House went farther and a little too far. Other candidates had been put up against Wilkes and one of these, though receiving a mere handful of votes, was declared elected. Naturally the country burst into furious indignation over this singularly barefaced outrage on the security of elections. Wilkes ending soon afterward, that is to say in April, 1770, his term of imprisonment, became the most popular man in England.

It is necessary to understand this situation to see how it appealed to and affected Chatterton. While the warfare was at its hottest he was pouring out a flood of metrical satires and prose articles, assailing with vindictive bitterness the government, the Dowager Princess of Wales (the king's mother), the beef-witted Duke of Grafton, even, so far as the prevailing conditions allowed, the dull king himself. For these effusions he presently found a ready and appreciative market in London, and in a short time he was sending them regularly to the *Freeholders' Magazine*, a periodical in Wilkes's interest.

They were worth all the attention they received and more, for in that storm and stress of politics appears now only one other light so clear as this; only one other among all the champions engaged in the controversy wrote more powerful English, and that one was the redoubtable Junius himself. An extraordinary power over bitter and sarcastic utterance made the boy a formidable warrior in these lists, and he had appeared but once or twice in the columns of the *Freeholders' Magazine* before the discerning editor was looking eagerly for the communications of "D. B. of Bristol."

Thus this boy, fifteen, sixteen years old, became one of the most ardent, zealous, and effective advocates of the democratic cause. It makes us smile now, that suggestion, because it seems so extravagant, and yet the fact is that by Wilkes and his friends, such as Beckford, Lord Mayor of London, the services of their Bristol lieutenant were recognized and prized when they had not the slightest suspicion that those clean shafts that went so far and shot so true were hurled by a slender apprentice in the office of a curmudgeon Bristol lawyer.

He carried on all together, Rowley in poetry and prose, Canynge, Barrett, two Catcotts, the lawyer's office, the precedents, the parchments, Wilkes, the king, Grafton, and the rest, and almost every night between eight and ten (for these were the hours of his liberty) he was at his mother's house. The history of the human mind reveals no other instance of an industry so prodigious and varied. Of these poems that have been preserved two full volumes are made, and his prose writings would easily fill a still larger volume, perhaps two, and this takes no account of his manuscripts that were destroyed at his death nor of the bulk of them that has otherwise perished. And all these works written in the space of about three years! The thing is not in nature. To produce in one year a poem so perfect as "Aella," so well considered, carefully wrought, and ably managed, would be an achievement; but the year that saw "Aella" written saw the making of many other poems in the pseudo-antique dialect and in modern form, and a variety of able prose writings as well, and still his labors at Lambert's conscientiously performed, his nightly visit to his mother and sister, his reading and studying, his unending quest for books and knowledge, his disputations with the Catcotts. On what theory of cellular activity shall we account for all these things?

He found time also to form a little circle of friends or acquaintances that had or were made to have an interest in literature, probably the boy's conception of the best he could do in Bristol to imitate the wit-gatherings at the Mermaid. The others of this company were, like Chatterton, called from employments ordinarily estranged from the muses. Thus Thomas Cary, one of the most promising among them, was by trade a maker of tobacco pipes, Henry Kator was a confectioner's apprentice, Mathew Mease was a vintner, and so on. It appears that under Chatterton's inspiration all of these became interested in experiments in verse or prose and all must have been equally inspired by the hot young radical to follow with attention the course of political events in their country. He made also some acquaintance with the two leading organists of Bristol, one Broderip and one Allen, for he was in love with music and transported whenever he heard it. He also made a practise of listening to various noted clergymen of the time and subsequently of satirizing and ridiculing their sermons. He spared not even the august Dr. Newton, Bishop of Bristol, to whom he addressed a letter, still extant in manuscript, savagely assailing the prelate's views on non-resistance, the supreme authority of the sovereign and other Tory tenets. A cordial invitation to the Bishop to excommunicate for heresy the writer of the letter is one of its interesting features, but the best sentences contain the boy's frank, eloquent defense of liberty. Dr. Newton had called John Wilkes "a blasphemer" for criticizing the king's ministers. "Turn over your own treatise on Revelation candidly," says Chatterton, "and tell me who is the most atrocious blasphemer, the man who denies the justice of God by maintaining the damnable doctrine of predestination, or he that justly ridicules the blunders, not the fundamentals of religion." His extreme freedom with his pen and his power of stinging sarcasm must have come home to some of his victims. One night when he was returning from his mother's house a man sprang upon him, knocked him down and beat him, cursing him and telling him he would "spoil his writing arm." No other explanation appears of this incident, which is the only case in which Chatterton appeared in a scene of violence and this without his will. But it was an age when a blow or a duel was taken to be adequate repartee. The Wilkes party had many friends in Bristol but it had also bitter enemies. Probably what happened was that Chatterton had in his biting fashion lampooned some of these and an aggrieved one responded after the manner of the times.

In that day the shade of Pope still ruled the realm of poesy, and to emulate the Dunciad was esteemed the crown of the poet's earthly glory. When one succeeded in adding to the dust heap of oblivion something in heroic couplets that had an epigrammatic flavor the polite world cheered joyously. There was no more poetry in the mass of this stuff than there is perfume in paper flowers, but from Dryden to Chatterton you will search mostly in vain for anything else. It is not the least of the marvels of Chatterton's story that in a time when the complacent verdict of the world had named one form as the supernal essence of poetic art he broke so far away and wrote in a style so different. But that was in the Rowley poems. His satires, being designed for immediate consumption and effect, followed more or less the taste of his times. Churchill, a rather clever rhymer of licentious predilections, was esteemed to have come nearest to the idol of the age. Most of Chatterton's satirical verses will be found to discount Churchill in wit and point and to be superior in aim. There has been preserved, unluckily, and incorporated with his poems, a mass of sketch-work with which from time to time he employed himself, as an artist makes idle hour studies, perhaps of leaves. But his serious efforts in political satire are worth attention as specimens of that not very valuable art.

One, at least, has a touch of sarcasm far beyond the average of such compositions. It is called "Resignation" and begins with a mock apostrophe to that virtue, and then proceeds to advise the Duke of Grafton, prime minister, to share its calm delights and gratify the country by resigning his office.

> Hail, Resignation! 'tis from thee we trace
> The various villanies of power and place;
> When rascals, once but infamy and rags,
> Rich with a nation's ruin, swell their bags,
> Purchase a title and a royal smile,
> And pay to be distinguishably vile;
> When big with self-importance thus they shine,
> Contented with their gleanings they resign!
> When ministers, unable to preside,
> The tottering vehicle no longer guide,

> The powerful Thane prepares to kick his Grace
> From all his glorious dignities of place;
> But still the honour of the action's thine,
> And Grafton's tender conscience can resign.
> Lament not, Grafton, that thy hasty fall
> Turns out a public happiness to all;
> Still by your emptiness of look appear
> The ruins of a man who used to steer;
> Still wear that insignificance of face,
> Which dignifies you more than power or place.

There are about eight hundred lines of this, some of them of no moment; but the savage characterization of Bute still possesses interest for the curious, and here and there are passages of strong poetic merit. It is remarkable and clearly shows his innate convictions that Chatterton was one of the earliest and most outspoken friends of the American Colonies. At the outset of their struggle, before the Boston tea-party, before the patriots had thought of independence, the cause that was presently to grow into revolution had stirred a profound sympathy in this boy's heart. Twice in "Resignation" he recurs to it.

> Alas! America, thy ruined cause
> Displays the ministry's contempt of laws.
> Unrepresented thou art tax'd, excised,
> By creatures much too vile to be despised;
> The outcasts of an ousted gang are sent
> To bless thy commerce with misgovernment.
> Whilst pity rises to behold thy fate,
> We see thee in this worst of troubles great;

> Whilst anxious for thy wavering dubious cause,
> We give thy proper spirit due applause.

The other reference is near the close:

> New to oppression and the servile chain,
> Hark how the wrong'd Americans complain.
> Whilst unregarded the petitions lie,
> And Liberty unnoticed swells her cry.

Some of these productions, like "Kew Gardens," he did not publish at once, but laid by for a future purpose that was slowly taking shape in his mind; some he gave to Catcott and some were obviously mere practise work, partly for the entertainment of himself and the friends of his little wit-circle and partly to keep his hand in for his grand design. In some of his verses he ranged through the court and camp of his day, letting fly at every head in sight, cabinet ministers, actors, pseudo-scientists, scurvy poets, noblemen, and particularly at Dr. Samuel Johnson, whose violent reactionary principles and natural arrogance of temper made him an irresistible target for one of Chatterton's republican faith and nimble wit. He ridiculed unsparingly Johnson's unlucky tragedy of "Irene," and repeatedly jabbed at the good doctor's critical pretensions. The number of eminent characters of his day that are brought into these verses is rather astonishing and shows how keenly he analyzed men and motives and how habituated he was to a close observation. His mind seemed to leap instantly to the salient characteristic of every man in the public eye, or to the weakest point in his armor. All the court party he lashed, but most he raged against Bute and Grafton. It was a time of much license in abusive speech — so long as one did not abuse the sacred majesty of the pin-head king — but the literature of the day reveals nothing more vitriolic than Chatterton's assaults upon these men. When he had made a dozen lines sufficiently contemptuous of the feudal champions he embalmed the matter in some poem and kept it by him ready to be lifted into action whenever occasion might demand. Thus many passages in "The Exhibition," an unpublished poem in the Bristol Museum, were transplanted to "Kew Gardens," and many others from "Kew Gardens" were reproduced in still another satire.

He was busy also with many poems in the modern manner other than satires. For some reason never explained his mind turned often toward Africa, and he composed, at different times, a series of African eclogues or semi-narratives in rhymed couplets, "Narva and Mored," "Heccar and Gaira," and "The Death of Nicou." He wrote on a great variety of subjects and in a great variety of meters. "The Copernican System" (he was then studying astronomy), "February, an Elegy," and the many songs, addresses, and elegiac verses indicate something of the vast range of his powers. I give a specimen of these songs — "The Invitation":

Away to the woodlands, away!
The shepherds are forming a ring,
To dance to the honour of May,
And welcome the pleasures of Spring.
The shepherdess labours a grace,
And shines in her Sunday's array,
And bears in the bloom of her face
The charms and the beauties of May.

    Away to the woodlands, away!
    The shepherds are forming a ring,
    To dance to the honour of May,
    And welcome the pleasures of Spring.

Away to the woodlands, away!
And join with the amorous train:
'Tis treason to labour to-day,
Now Bacchus and Cupid must reign.
With garlands of primroses made,
And crown'd with the sweet blooming spray,
Through woodland, and meadow, and shade,
We'll dance to the honour of May.

    Away to the woodlands, away!
    And join with the amorous train:
    'Tis treason to labour to-day,
    Now Bacchus and Cupid must reign.

He had a neat hand at the kind of love verses that were then esteemed the very flower of elegant wit, and produced a deal of them, counting those he made for his friend Baker to send to the beauteous Miss Hoyland and all he made on his own account to "Miss Burt, of Bristol," "Miss Clarke," "Miss C—"

and so on.   He could write these things with a free
soul, for it appears that while he liked the society of
intelligent women and admired the sex he never was
genuinely in love in his life, perhaps from lack of
time. He also dealt in clever little pastorals and
idyls after the manner of an age much given to metrical fripperies of this sort, but the odd fact is that in
almost everything he wrote from grave to gay is a
finished and masterly workmanship, and very often
are lines that glow with the immortal fire in spite of
their tawdry surroundings. The acknowledged poems
being mostly mere momentary effusions, or else
pot-boilers and hence of necessity in the debased
style then current, are greatly inferior to the Rowley
poems in which his genius had full wing-room
to soar, and his infallible perceptions about art led
him untrammeled beyond the comprehension of
those dull times; but even the acknowledged poems
have a certain merit.   For instance, the elegies on the
death of his old friend the usher Phillips have genuine feeling; the humorous verses have a clever
diabolical wit, and occasional passages in the satires
show a poetic substance entirely above and away
from the subject.   As take in the unpublished poem,
"The Exhibition," the two lines (quoted by Dr.
Gregory), referring to a celebrated organist of Bristol:

> "He keeps the passions with the sound in play
> And the soul trembles with the trembling key."

And the like flashes of beauty show here and there in other poems that are in themselves of little worth. Finally it may be noted that while he studied no Latin at Colston's and knew of it only what he had been able to gather by his unaided efforts, he essayed, with the help of a literal version, to make metrical translations of two of Horace's Odes, and did them not badly. A series of prose romances purporting to be taken from ancient Saxon or ancient British sources is added to but does not complete the list of his performances.

Always amid these pursuits his cherished plan was maturing and he saw now that the time was at hand to put it into operation. The lawyer's office had become to his spirit an inexpressible burden. Lambert was a Gradgrind of a kind certain to produce revolt in any lad both sensitive and proud. As I have said, Chatterton made it a practise to visit his mother and sister almost every night. Lambert's office closed at eight o'clock. He was obliged to be in his employer's house by ten, so he had two hours for his visit. He was so fond of the little family that he would sometimes linger a moment beyond the time, or perhaps his mother would detain him, and then he would arise in haste, saying that he must go to get the scolding that he knew was in store for him. This Lambert was, in truth, a brutal person. He had little business, so Chatterton had in the office much time that was necessarily unoccupied in service; but Lambert violently objected to any use the boy made of this time. First he forbade his apprentice to write on the office stationery. As Chatterton received no wages this was near to be an embargo on his singing until Mrs. Edkins came to his relief and gave him a little money. Instead of appeasing Lambert this seemed to anger him the more.

"How did you get that paper?" he thundered when he discovered Chatterton to be writing.

"Very honestly," said Chatterton proudly.

Lambert snatched it from his hand, tore it to bits and flung it into his face. Subsequently the lawyer discovered in a desk both Chatterton's store of white paper and many of his completed manuscripts. These he ruthlessly destroyed. Chatterton complained to Mrs. Edkins that in this way some of his poems had been hopelessly lost. The letters to his friends that Lambert had torn up he could easily rewrite, he said, but the poems were gone forever.

Yet the boy was a faithful servant to the tyrant. There are still in existence three hundred and seventy-four closely written foolscap pages of law precedents neatly copied in Chatterton's careful hand to attest his industry. He was punctual and obedient, and although Lambert feared and disliked him in about equal degrees, he could find no other fault with him than that "there was no way to keep boys from idling," — idling in the Lambert vocabulary meaning to write poetry or to study when there was no office work to be done. Lambert used to send the footman to spy on the apprentice, being under some suspicion that Chatterton might leave the office when there was nothing to do, but the footman always found him at his post.

Sometimes at home Chatterton told Mrs. Edkins that Lambert's tyranny and meanness were unbearable, and he threatened to run away. In 1770 that would have meant the bridewell, for so the law dealt with fugitive apprentices. Mrs. Edkins remonstrated with him, and asked why he should do a thing so wrong and so certain to cause trouble for him. To go to London, the boy said, to get money to help his mother and sister.

He seemed to Mrs. Edkins, who was his godmother, to be never in spirits but always with a grave, serious, studying face, full of thought and concern. Sometimes at Lambert's he would not say a word, unless he were spoken to, for two days together, and then with his face cleared up he would take aside one of his young friends and read or repeat one of the Rowley poems upon which he had been engrossed. In other words, when he seemed to be morose he was merely intent upon a work in hand. As a specimen of the treatment he has had I may mention that it is customary to cite the fact of his

periodical and pensive silences but never to refer to
the cause.   Apparently, it is thought that while he
was meditating his artistry he should have been skip-
ping the rope or making merry with his comrades.

It was impossible that such a connection as that
between the small-souled lawyer and the aspiring
poet should endure, for its path led straight to trouble.
Moreover, there came now voices that the boy heard,
and they summoned him to London and another
career.   The editors of the *Middlesex Journal*
and of the *Town and Country Magazine* had praised
his writings and hinted that if he cared to come to
London he might do well, and at that dulcet sound
he strained hard against the chains that bound him
to Bristol.   To be perched upon a stool in a dingy
office copying dull precedents, practising by stealth
and at odd moments the art that was the breath of
his life, was a barren existence to one that was both
a dreamer of dreams and fired with a mounting
ambition.   But he was bound by his articles, he was
an apprenticed slave; unless the crusty attorney
could be induced to cancel his indenture he had no
hope of freedom.

In these straits he matured an ingenious but wicked
device, and yet one quite naturally suggested by his
musings and his habitual melancholy.   No doubt
Chatterton, like Shelley, to whom he was strangely
akin, had considered suicide until he reached the

conclusion that in certain conditions to end one's life is not only innocent but laudable. That scene in Trelawney's "Records," where Shelley proposes to leap from an open boat and "solve the great mystery," had an odd parallel when Chatterton one evening after discoursing of suicide to some friends drew a pistol from his pocket and pointing it to his forehead exclaimed, "Ah, if one had but the courage to pull the trigger!" Now a misadventure with a letter of his gave a clue to the way from his prison. A friend of his in Bristol was one Michael Clayfield, a well-to-do distiller and the owner of many books, among which Chatterton had browsed delightedly. He wrote occasionally to Clayfield and dedicated poems to him, and one of the letters, in which he advocated suicide and suggested his intention to take his own life, he accidentally left upon his desk. Lambert, who seems to have been, in a characteristic way, prying about to see how his apprentice spent his time, came upon and read this document. He sent it to Barrett, who says he lectured Chatterton on the horrid sin of self-destruction until the boy wept, a triumph of eloquence of which the surgeon's contemporaries would hardly have believed him capable. But at least here was the way open and the slave of precedents lost no time in preparing another and similar document that should be more useful to his purposes.

On April 15, 1770, Chatterton being then seventeen years and five months old, the spying Lambert found on his apprentice's desk a paper bearing the startling title, "The Last Will and Testament of Thomas Chatterton," and reading on discovered it to be an intending suicide's farewell to the world. "All this wrote between 11 and 2 o'clock Saturday, in the utmost distress of mind, April 14, 1770," it began, and continued with a metrical address to his friends and other matter, running into this explicit statement:

"*Item.* If, after my death, which will happen to-morrow night before eight o'clock, being the Feast of the Resurrection, the coroner and jury bring it in lunacy, I will and direct that Paul Farr, Esq., and Mr. John Flower, at their joint expense, cause my body to be interred in the tomb of my fathers, and raise the monument over my body to the height of four feet five inches, placing the present flat stone on the top, and adding six tablets." Inscriptions for these tablets followed; five were heraldic and satirical and only one has any present appeal to the minds of men:

"TO THE MEMORY OF

THOMAS CHATTERTON

Reader, judge not. If thou art a Christian, believe
that he shall be judged by a supreme power: to that
power alone he is now answerable."

The lawyer was, after his nature, properly shocked by his discovery, but there was in fact nothing to alarm the judicious. A more discerning mind would have been on the whole rather moved to interest and mild amusement, for many passages showed that the apprentice had no possible design upon his life.

"*Item*. I give all my vigor and fire of youth to Mr. George Catcott, being sensible he is most in want of it.

"*Item*. From the same charitable motive, I give and bequeath unto the Rev. Mr. Camplin, sen., all my humility. To Mr. Burgum all my prosody and grammar, likewise one moiety of my modesty, the other moiety to any young lady who can prove, without blushing, that she wants that valuable commodity. . . . I leave also my religion to Dr. Cutts Barton, Dean of Bristol, hereby empowering the sub-sacrist to strike him on the head when he goes to sleep in church. . . .

"*Item*. I leave all my debts, the whole not five pounds, to the payment of the charitable and generous Chamber of Bristol, on penalty, if refused, to hinder every member from a good dinner by appearing in the form of a bailiff."

And so on. Certainly a man does not write like this on the eve of destroying himself. But Lambert had long been in awe of his strange young apprentice; his mother, who managed his household, was thoroughly convinced her lodger was crazy, and a kind of panic terror fell upon them lest Chatterton should kill himself before he could be gotten off the premises. They must have passed a sleepless Sunday night, housed with a dangerous lunatic that had openly proclaimed his purpose to lay violent hands upon himself. On Monday morning, April 16, the indentures were hastily canceled and without more ado Chatterton found himself released from the hateful servitude to precedents and free to tread the path where the lights shone and the voices called.

He set straightway about it, having long turned over in his mind all these contingencies and how he should act therein. One week he took to prepare for his setting forth and to say farewells. His Bristol friends made up a little purse for his expenses — a few pounds all told. Clayfield contributed gladly, no doubt; the Catcotts gave something, Cary added a little, and it has even been supposed that on this occasion an unwonted fire thawed the chill breast of Barrett; a kindly but probably a strained imagining. He went about his farewells with the utmost cheerfulness. To his mother and sister he was all tender consolation. One of his characteristic performances was to gather a group of children on the steps of St. Mary Redcliffe and bringing up gingerbread from a shop across the street and near his mother's house, give them a farewell banquet on this national

dainty. Other youths or even men in like fashion
approaching from the country that fierce struggle in
the great city have had sinking of heart and been
shaken of vague alarms. From the beginning this
boy had looked with entire self-possession upon the
seething combat and the part he should play in it.
Seventeen years old, and equipped with nothing but
his two hands and what scanty education he had
picked from the stony field of a commercial school,
he marched without a tremor. London had no
terrors for him, of no man alive was he afraid. A
brave, cool spirit, full of the courage that comes of
weighing causes and reasoning of foundation matters,
he looked with unconcern upon the desperate chances
of that venture. He knew the world, he knew men,
he knew that his own address never failed to win him
respect and attention, and he was not deceived about
the divine fire that he bore. He knew he bore it, he
knew that of all the men of his generation he had been
singled out to be the message bringer.

His farewells were made, his clothing was prepared
for him by his mother and sister, and a week after
Lambert had dismissed him, that is to say, on Mon-
day, April 23, 1770, he sat on the coach bound for
London and bowling down the curving road to Bath.
He was not plunging quite unfriended into the great
city. A relative of his, a kind of cousin, one Mrs.
Ballance, lodged in the house of a friendly plasterer

in Shoreditch and thither he was bound.   It rained
that day and he sat inside most of the way, and that
night snow fell heavily and on Marlborough Downs
the snow was near a foot deep.   His facility in
making acquaintances and winning friendships had
exercise in the coach.   His fellow-traveler beside
him was a Quaker, a journeyman wood-carver, who,
before Bath was reached, became so much interested
in the youth that he would fain have gone to London
to be in his company, only he had not his tools.
The next day was clear and cold and he sat beside
the driver, and that seasoned observer of the world
and mankind was won with the rest, telling the boy
he sat bolder and tighter than any other person that
had ridden with him.   But so it was always: few
could look upon that face without being strangely
moved by it, either to obvious admiration and liking,
as was the honest "Gee-ho" of the stage-coach, or to
a vague unrest and concern, as was the curmudgeon
lawyer.

He reached London at five o'clock in the afternoon of April 25, the journey of one hundred and
eighteen miles then occupying the better part of two
days.   At Shoreditch he found his cousin and got
lodgings with the honest plasterer, being in fact,
bedmate of the plasterer's nephew.   His two prime
traits, tireless energy and his tender home feeling, were
instantly displayed.   Within twenty-four hours of his

arrival he had seen four of the men from whom he
expected to win fame and fortune, had settled his
plans for work, and had written to his mother a letter
full of cheer. The four men he had seen were
Edmunds, editor of the *Middlesex Journal*, in Shoe
Lane, Holborn; Hamilton of the *Town and Country
Magazine* at St. John's Gate, Clerkenwell; Fell
of the *Freeholders' Magazine*, in Paternoster Row;
and James Dodsley, the book-seller of Pall Mall and
the recipient of his letters about "Aella." To all
except Dodsley he was very well known by name.
Fell was one of the leaders of the Wilkes party;
Edmunds was of the same faith; to both their periodicals Chatterton had contributed often. The
Town and Country Magazine had printed many
of his miscellanies. The astonishment that fell upon
these men when they found that the writer of those
rattling letters on politics, of those vigorous metrical
satires, was a slip of a boy with a grave calm face and
preternaturally bright eyes must have exceeded anything in their experience. The same impression that
he had made elsewhere attended him here. There
was that in his dignified bearing, his manifest intelligence and his manner, at once frank and engaging, that instantly forestalled any thought of treating
him as a boy. The graybeards made way for him;
boy and all he had his place at the front of the
fight.

"Great encouragement from them; all approved
of my design," he wrote his mother when he returned
to Shoreditch that day.   His design was to establish
himself as a writer, and indeed it looked probable
enough.   No other mind in England, save only the
mysterious Junius, possessed such a compelling
power upon words.   The time, too, was urgent,
being electric with the premonitions of the vivifying
storms of the French revolution.   Periodical literature was in its beginning, active inquiry was on foot
about divine right and government, and above all the
forces were arrayed in London for the great struggle
between people and throne over Wilkes and Beckford.

Beckford was lord mayor.   He was of acute mind
and a ready courage, many sterling qualities of
leadership, a sincere love of democracy, and he was
re-inforced by the knowledge of a great popular
majority behind him.   Six days before Chatterton
reached London Wilkes had ended his twenty-two
months' imprisonment for speaking disrespectfully of
the king, and London was still ringing with the en-
thusiastic celebration of his release.   Beckford was
of Wilkes's turn of mind.   The right of electors to
choose whom they would without interference from
the crown was the vital issue in the case of Wilkes,
and under the leadership of Beckford the corporation of London presented to the king a petition that
the sanctity of elections be maintained.   It was a

movement purely on Wilkes's behalf and therefore
ruffled the king's temper.   He did not like it because
he detested Wilkes and all that Wilkes stood for,
and he had no more wit than to reply to it in a spirit
of quarrel.   It gave him great concern, said this dull
monarch, to find that any of his subjects "should
have been so far misled as to offer me an address
and remonstrance, the contents of which I cannot
but consider as disrespectful to me, injurious to my
parliament, and irreconcilable to the principles of
the constitution."   This was bad enough, but what
inflamed the populace to a perilous wrath was that
when the king had read to Beckford's deputation this
unmannerly speech he made an open jest of the affair
to the leaders of the court party that were with him.
To be jested about is usually the intolerable burden
to men that have a serious cause, and for the cause
that Beckford represented thrones have been shaken
down and kings' heads have rolled in the sawdust.
London was in no mood for laughter; it immediately
made Wilkes an alderman to spite the court party
and settled into a dogged contest to secure the debated
seat in Parliament.

Wilkes and Beckford meantime planned another
deputation to the king, and on May 23 an audience
was granted.   Beckford, of course, headed the party
and read the petition, which was a spirited remonstrance against the king's churlish response to the

former address. That is, it was held in that day to be extremely spirited and dangerously bold. A later generation would have choked at the expressions of humility wherewith it was plentifully larded. But it remonstrated, that was the main thing, and it hit hard the foolish king, for as soon as it concluded George III pulled out his reply, which was even more exasperating and ill-conceived than his previous effort had been. But Beckford was ready, having probably understood clearly from the beginning what would be the outcome of the visit. Before the monarch could move away the mayor had burst into a brief but pointed extemporaneous harangue in which, with every expression of loyal devotion to the king and the government, he contrived to rap George over the knuckles for his attitude towards the people. Whoever had dared, said Beckford, to alienate the king's affections from his loyal subjects in general and from the city of London in particular was "an enemy to your majesty's person and family, a violator of the public peace, and a betrayer of our happy constitution as it was established at the glorious Revolution."

Tremendous excitement followed this daring outburst, and Beckford was hailed everywhere with wondering applause as one that had ventured single-handed into a lion's den and come out unbitten. To speak thus to a king and escape the vengeful bolts of heaven was as if the days of miracles had returned.

Beckford became a popular idol and a fixed star among the nation's heroes, his bold deed being to this day emblazoned on his statue in the Guildhall.

This was the storm center into which Chatterton projected himself and where he was become in four weeks a figure of consequence. Beckford knew him personally and liked him; Wilkes knew his work very well, and told Fell it was simply impossible that such writings should come from a boy of eighteen years and he was eager to meet such a marvel. There was some understanding of active cooperation between Beckford and Chatterton that has never been cleared up. In one of the letters, filled with cheering and loving messages, that the boy wrote home, he intimated something of the kind but not the extent to which he took part in the popular party's affairs. "You have doubtless heard of the Lord Mayor's remonstrating and addressing the king," he says, "but it will be a piece of news to inform you that I have been with the Lord Mayor on the occasion." He describes briefly his first meeting with Beckford and adds, "The rest is a secret." It has remained a secret, but the popular leaders were only too glad to have the assistance of the terrible flail of that pen.

VI

Now Cracks a Noble Heart

So far as that he had won his upward path. It was an age not partial to boys. Then and for generations afterward, the lot of children in the world was hard enough. The dullard time seemed to revenge itself for its own shortcomings by making the utmost of the scant superiority of years. To be seen seldom and to be heard not at all, to be regarded as enemies of adult peace and complacency, was only part of the iron rule for childhood. Dotheboys Hall was a sadly true picture and it came in a later and gentler time. To know the horrid and tolerated cruelty meted out in the eighteenth century to boys, as to those in the navy, for instance, is to have your blood boil at the senseless tyranny. Boys seemed to be made to be beaten, to be frowned upon, suppressed and disliked. Yet in four weeks this boy had won a man's place among the leaders of his party. Almost his first step on reaching London had been made in characteristic fashion toward that acquaintance with Beckford of which I have spoken. He wrote to the lord mayor a letter of warm congratulation upon the first remonstrance and followed the letter in person. Beckford received him with wonder, no doubt, but quickly perceived that he was dealing with no ordinary mind. Indeed, the polished address, the gravity and self-possession, the extraordinary command of language, the evidences of thought and wide acquaintance with affairs, were irresistible. The mayor was exceedingly affable, and when the boy offered to write another letter further endorsing the policy of the remonstrance Beckford readily enough approved and was evidently sensible that the gods had raised for him a champion of unusual gifts. The letter was written and the leaders arranged to have it published as a broadside in the revived *North Briton.*

But all this, of course, had little or nothing to do with the boy's inner life. In Shoreditch was his cousin, Mrs. Ballance, but neither there nor elsewhere was the kind of companionship that would have been most serviceable to him, the sympathetic understanding of his nature and aims, the interest that perceives and would fain help. In the midst of the throngs of London he was more truly alone than he had been in Bristol. Mrs. Ballance had expected, doubtless, to find a boy like the rest of the Chattertons she had known. She was startled and nonplussed, poor woman, to come upon a genius in her own family. One scrap of their conversation is preserved. When he came in she called him "Cousin Tommy," for he seemed to her but a little boy.

He drew himself up with indignant pride.

"Don't call me Tommy," he said sharply.

"Why not?" said the good woman, perplexed. "That is your name, isn't it?"

"Did you ever know a poet named *Tommy?*" said the boy in great scorn.

Mrs. Ballance could make nothing of him. All he seemed to care to talk about was Wilkes, the popular revolt, and political matters that were truly Greek to her. Once he frightened her into the border land of hysteria by announcing that he hoped presently to be sent to the Tower. In all her recollections no Chatterton had ever been sent to the Tower. He told her that he expected to settle the state of the nation, and probably enjoyed the wide-mouthed wonder which with she received the information. He seemed to her hardly human in his way of life. He cared nothing about food, which argued an abnormal constitution and one that filled his cousin with dismay. He was supposed to board with her, but his boarding was something like the feeding of a bird. He had always been (like Shelley again) exceedingly abstemious in this regard. Animal food he usually rejected on his old theory that it impaired the clear working of his intellect. A tart and a glass of water were a dinner for him. He never drank wine nor liquor, and his capacity for unremitting toil amazed the simple folk around him. The plasterer's nephew thought his roommate a kind of demon, agreeable enough, but still a demon, for he sat writing and studying far into the night, and early in the morning he was again at toil. He seemed never to sleep and seldom to eat. The nephew saw him once or twice take a sheep's tongue from his pocket and make a luncheon upon it, barely intermitting his labor even for the slight repast. The record of his ceaseless activities seems incredible. The writing he produced in those days for only its extent and its variety of subject would be among the mysteries of literature. Few authors in any age and in any length of time have covered a greater range. Pleasure he hardly knew the name of. If he went to the theater or the fashionable gardens, or to the Chapter Coffee House, it was to gather material for his interminable work. Bright-eyed he walked the crowded streets looking incessantly for the things he was to write about. A tremendous ambition consumed him; he saw the fame and success he had dreamed about almost within his reach, and between the little room in Shoreditch and the publishing offices he toiled back and forth like a driven slave.

He was, indeed, a slave to the publishers of the day. For almost every known periodical in London

he was a contributor. Everything that went to press
was (to reverse the ancient phrase) a mill for his
grist. To the *Middlesex Journal* and the *Freeholders' Magazine* he contributed political essays; in
Hamilton's *Town and Country Magazine*, in the
London, the *Court and City*, and *Gospel Magazines*,
the *London Museum* and the *Political Register* he had
many miscellanies in prose and verse. I put the
Town and Country first because with that, and with
Hamilton the editor thereof, he had most to do.
In this periodical appeared a series of eleven clever
sketches of contemporaneous life, mostly written in the
character of an observer about town. Some of these,
the letters of "Tony Selwood" for instance, are
touched with a keen observation and clear understanding of human nature and some show evidences
of a strong narrative power. Many of his writings
were pot-boilers, and one paper, the story of "Maria
Friendless," was a paraphrase of a tale of Johnson's
in the *Rambler*. Yet it is impossible to deny that
pot-boilers or otherwise, they were well done. The
tone of literature in that day was licentious. Things
were printed in the most respectable magazines that
to-day could not be printed anywhere. Writing for
daily bread and naturally not much concerned about
permanent value in productions so ephemeral and
commercial, Chatterton often followed in his themes
the prevailing fashions. The periodicals he wrote for

were the best of his day, and these things were
then taken as a matter of course, but some of his
papers reprinted in a later age have served to further
in an undeserved way the reputation that has been
manufactured for him of libertinism. "The Memoirs of a Sad Dog" are not edifying reading; yet
they are no worse than many other sketches that were
appearing in the magazines. The productive tide
was swollen, too, from the work of past days. From
his trunk came forth many things that had budded
in Lambert's dingy office and had escaped, for the
use now found, the destroying fingers of the lawyer;
such things as so-called translations of Saxon poems,
tales and articles, and he even sent to his sister for
the glossary he had invented for Rowley, heralding
renewed activities by that excellent poet.

His trade as a satirist in prose and verse gave him
an opportunity to express his opinion of Horace
Walpole, and the way he availed himself of it made
history. Again and again he slashed the noble lord
with the keenest blade that shone in those times.
In the satirical poem "Kew Gardens," in the prose
"Memoirs of a Sad Dog" and elsewhere, Walpole
repeatedly figures in the most ridiculous light as the
"Baron Otranto." In one of the "Sad Dog" papers
the attack is particularly ingenious, since it takes
the earl on his most vulnerable side, his posing as
a dilettante scientist and antiquarian. Chatterton

represents him as visiting at a country house, where
in the dog kennel he discovers a stone with letters
engraved upon it. It is in fact a piece of an old tombstone that has fallen to such base uses that it now
keeps the dogs from crawling through a hole in the
wall; but the Baron Otranto is certain that he has
found an ancient relic of great value, and after days
of solitary study announces that he has deciphered
the inscription. It means, he says, that the
place where he found it was the tomb of an old
British saint of renown; whereas it is really
the gravestone of honest Bill Hicks. Walpole could
never have seen the savage reference in "Kew Gardens" to his foolish performance with Kitty Clive,
the actress, for whom he built a house at Twicken-
ham, but what he did see was enough. The sar-
casms were done in that bitter, lancet-edged style of
which Chatterton was the master, and might have
cut to the quick the toughest hide. Walpole's was
not of that kind; like all men that are unsure of themselves and cover their deficiencies by posing, he was
particularly sensitive to ridicule. Years afterward,
when the author of "Kew Gardens" was dead,
the attention drawn to his works completed his revenge for the insult Walpole had put upon him,
and under the torture Walpole writhed as much as
might be desired. But it was a costly revenge, for
the boy being dead and that powerful pen of his at

rest, the man was at perfect liberty to assail him in any way he pleased, and the way he chose stained Chatterton's reputation for more than a century.

Five of his political essays were printed in the *Middlesex Journal* in the month of May. One of them was addressed to the Earl of Hillsborough, the Minister of Colonies, who was held largely responsible for the troubles in America; one to the king's mother, the Princess Dowager of Wales, whose shadow continued to fall more or less on her son's unhappy reign; one to North, then Prime Minister, and one to the Electors of Bristol. The Hillsborough letter is to us the most interesting; I take an extract from it to show what were his sympathies for America and at the same time the strength of the weapon he wielded:

"My Lord, — If a constant exercise of tyranny and cruelty has not steeled your heart against all sensations of compunction and remorse, permit me to remind you of the recent massacre in Boston. It is an infamous attribute of the ministry of the Thane [1] that what his tools begin in secret fraud and oppression ends in murder and avowed assassination. Not contented to deprive us of our liberty, they rob us of our lives, knowing from a sad experience that the one without the other is an insupportable burden. Your lordship has bravely distinguished yourself

[1] He means Bute.

among the ministers of the present reign. Whilst
North and the instruments of his royal mistress
settled the plan of operation, it was your part to
execute; you were the assassin whose knife was ever
ready to finish the crime. If every feeling of hu-
manity is not extinct in you, reflect, for a moment
reflect, on the horrid task you undertook and per-
petrated," etc.

In the *Political Register* were printed his first letter
to Beckford and "The Prophecy," a vigorous
political appeal; in the *Freeholders' Magazine* for
May appeared the first part of the satirical poem
"Resignation" of which I have before spoken; in
the *London Museum* for May "Narva and Mored,"
one of his African eclogues, and in the June number
"The Death of Nicou," another of the same series;
in the *Town and Country Magazine* appeared an
elegy of his, "Maria Friendless," "The False Step"
(a prose story), an "Anecdote of Judge Jeffries,"
"To Miss Burt of Bristol" (a sentimental poem),
and his "Hunter of Oddities" papers; in the *Gospel*,
the *Court and City*, the *London* and other magazines
were many short contributions from his pen that have
never been recovered, so that we have here but an
imperfect list of his labors.

He was also busy in other directions to further his
interests and to extend his acquaintance. The Mermaid Tavern of his day was the Chapter Coffee House

in Paternoster Row, and he went there frequently until he was a figure somewhat familiar to its literary circle. He was at pains to dress well, to frequent places of fashionable resort, the theater and the gardens. He made acquaintances on. all sides, some that helped his harvesting, and what was remarkable in a young fellow first from home, none, so far as we know, that was injurious to him.

The publishers were eager to have his contributions; they were not eager to pay for them. It was the dawn of periodical literature, the magazines had small circulation and small profits; most of them, accordingly, depended for their matter upon the gratuitous offerings of ambitious writers. Few magazines had any commercial basis or were conducted as business enterprises; the whole vast field of advertising was yet to be discovered and developed, the magazines were the growth of vanity, whim, or political fervor. When contributions were paid for it was at a rate that seems to us mere match money. Yet this boy was making headway and his hope was high. The appreciation that he had received did not turn his head nor unduly exalt his spirits, and he labored steadily and intelligently toward his goal.

He wrote home regularly and always in a cheerful vein. As he made money he laid aside something of

the little income for presents for the family on Redcliffe Hill, remembering the grandmother with some
of her favorite tobacco and buying gifts of china-
ware and apparel for his mother and sister. He
assured them constantly that they should share his
success and he would provide for them every comfort. The whole wealth of an affectionate nature
was often poured out in these letters; no trace of irri-
tation or concern appeared in them; they had only
good news and terms of affection. Usually they are
in a style of sprightly good humor. He wrote to
his mother this:

SHOREDITCH, LONDON: May 6, 1770.

DEAR MOTHER, — I am surprised that no letter has been
sent in answer to my last. I am settled, and in such a settlement
as I would desire. I get four guineas a week by one magazine;
shall engage to write a history of England and other pieces, which
will more than double that sum. Occasional essays for the daily
papers would more than support me. What a glorious prospect!
Mr. Wilkes knew me by my writings since I first corresponded
with the book-sellers here. I shall visit him next week, and by
his interest will ensure Mrs. Ballance the Trinity house. He
affirmed that what Mr. Fell had of mine could not be the writings
of a youth, and expressed a desire to know the author. By the
means of another book-seller, I shall be introduced to Townshend
and Sawbridge. I am quite familiar at the Chapter Coffee
House, and know all the geniuses there. A character is now
unnecessary; an author carries his character in his pen. My
sister will improve herself in drawing. My grandmother is, I
hope, well. Bristol's mercenary walls were never destined to

hold me; there I was out of my element; now I am in it.   London!
— Good God!   How superior is London to that despicable place,
Bristol!   Here is none of your little meannesses, none of your
mercenary securities, which disgrace that miserable hamlet.
Dress, which is in Bristol an eternal fund of scandal, is here only
introduced as a subject of praise: if a man dresses well, he has
taste; if careless, he has his own reasons for so doing, and is prudent.   Need I remind you of the contrast?   The poverty of
authors is a common observation, but not always a true one.   No
author can be poor who understands the arts of book-sellers: without this necessary knowledge the greatest genius may starve, and
with it the greatest dunce live in splendour.   This knowledge I
have pretty well dipped into. — The Levant, man-of-war, in which
T. Wensley[1] went out, is at Portsmouth; but no news of him yet.
I lodge in one of Mr. Walmsley's best rooms.   Let Mr. Cary copy
the letters on the other side, and give them to the persons for
whom they are designed, if not too much labour for him. —

I remain yours and so forth,

T. CHATTERTON.

P. S. — I have some trifling presents for my mother, sister,
Thorne, et cetera.

The character of the boy shone out in his reference to his intentions about Mrs. Ballance as well
as in the "trifling presents."   His first natural impulse if he gained anything was to use it for some one
else.   His influence with his great friends he purposed to bend for Mrs. Ballance's benefit to secure
for her the Trinity House pension for the widows of
seamen in the navy.

[1] This was an acquaintance of the Chattertons.

By early June he was well established, his path
seemed clear to him, his earnings though small were
sufficient for his slender needs, and there seemed
every promise that his dream would be realized.   He
saw himself on the verge of all that he had desired,
fame and independence within his grasp, Rowley to
be given to the world, the work that was his life
recognized and praised.   And then, of a sudden, a
series of disasters arose to crush one by one the
fabric of his hopes.   Reaction and absolutism, without warning, thrust out their power and the boy was
caught in the falling walls of their overturning.
Parliament, after weeks of fierce discussion of the
Wilkes case, adjourned for the summer holidays
without deciding it.   Many of the leaders on both
sides left town, Wilkes himself went to the seashore,
the long hard battle came to a temporary pause, and
the government seized the opportunity to move in
relentless fashion upon its enemies.   The blows fell
in rapid succession. Edmunds, of the *Middlesex
Journal*, was arrested and sentenced to Newgate
Prison.   Fell, of the *Freeholders' Magazine*, was silenced and ruined by being thrust into King's Bench
jail on a trumped-up affair of debt.   Woodfall, of
the *Public Advertiser*, the publisher of Junius, was
haled before the King's Bench; Almon, of the *London
Museum*, before Lord Mansfield in Westminster Hall.
Miller, of the *London Evening Post*, was arrested

for the mere reprinting of a letter of Junius. Uncontrollable terror fell upon the opposition press; in a moment the voice of revolt was stifled; the democratic campaign came to an abrupt end, the editors and publishers still out of jail took warning and scrupulously purified their columns of the slightest word of dissent, and for the time being progress turned backward.

At one stroke, therefore, the greater part of Chatterton's market disappeared. All his friends and associates were in jail, or in flight, or silenced. It may be believed that there never was a braver heart. The blow he took full in the face and instantly he prepared to retrieve it. Writing to his sister of these events he declared that they would in the end be to his benefit, for the magazines would still be published, though their editors were in jail, and the demand for his work would be the greater. But he must have known better; he must have known, in fact, how the structure of his fortunes tottered, for he now set about enlarging the field of his employments.

The triumph of reaction and the overwhelming of the opposition were not all; it was Fell that was to bring Chatterton and Wilkes together, and Fell was now in prison. Chatterton had counted much on the introduction and doubtless saw how he could utilize it to his advantage, and now it was suddenly taken from him. Yet worse remained behind. In the midst of his misfortunes and the defeats of his party, Beckford still stood, the invincible, that looked upon the king and unterrified spoke his mind, Beckford from whom he confidently expected to have advancement. And suddenly, Beckford died. For a moment at this culminating misfortune the boy's steady self-command gave way. He stormed up and down Mrs. Ballance's room at Shoreditch, declaring that he was ruined, and all was over with him. The good Ballance was astonished at his agitation, which, knowing nothing of the understanding between the boy and the mayor, seemed unaccountable to her. The storm passed and once more he sat down sternly to outface disaster. He turned the death of his friend to immediate account by writing elegies and essays upon him, and these he managed to sell. The second letter to Beckford, which had been accepted by Bingley's *North Briton*, and was all but to fill the next issue of that revived periodical, was now of necessity returned to him, an additional blow to his prospects and a loss of almost two pounds in money. Outside he showed an unshaken front. To his friend Cary, in Bristol, he made light of the misfortune of Beckford's death by writing for him the following memorandum:

"Accepted by Bingley, set for, and thrown out of, the *North Briton*, 21st June, on account of Lord Mayor's death:

	£	s	d
Lost by his death on this Essay	1	11	6
Gained in Elegies	2	2	0
Gained in Essays	3	3	0
	5	5	0

Am glad he is dead by...

£ 3 13 6 "

But he was under no deception as to the situation he fronted and with desperation he fought for every chance. Among the acquaintances he had made (this time in the pit of Drury Lane Theater) was a young man connected with a music publisher's house in Cheapside. When he learned that Chatterton could write, this young man put him in the way of writing songs to be set to music and introduced him to a composer. Soon he had the satisfaction of hearing some of his songs sung in public at the gardens, and while the income from this source was very small it was a guide-post to a more promising field. One of the three popular summer gardens then in operation in London was the Marylebone. It was here that Chatterton heard his songs in the part of the entertainment (a kind of primitive vaudeville) that was given from the stage, promenading to the music of the band being the other attraction. While at Bristol he had begun and thrown aside a burlesque operetta that he now conceived would be available for use at this resort. He had called it "Amphitryon" and made it somewhat heavier than London taste called for. This now came out of his trunk and underwent a speedy recasting. "The Revenge" he rechristened it. The story turns on the wrath of Juno at the discovery that Jupiter has gone love-making after Maia. It is exceedingly funny, the quarreling of Jupiter and Juno being managed with great spirit and cleverness; very easily one may see how with equally effective music the thing would go with immense effect. A swift succession of songs in different quick-footed meters gives the whole a sur-passingly lively air. The songs are interspersed with short recitatives; the whole thing is in verse. I will give a taste of its quality by quoting the beginning of the first act:

> *Jupiter* (recitative)
> I swear by Styx, the usage is past bearing;
> My lady Juno ranting, tearing, swearing!
> Why, what the devil will my godship do,
> If blows and thunder cannot tame a shrew?

> *Air*
> Tho' the loud thunder rumbles,
> Tho' storms rend the sky;
> Yet louder she grumbles,
> And swells the sharp cry.

> Her jealousy teasing,
> Disgusting her form;
> Her music as pleasing
> As pigs in a storm.

I fly her embraces,
To wenches more fair;
And leave her wry faces,
Cold sighs and despair.

Cupid comes to tell Juno that her lord has gone
to meet Maia.

Juno

How! What! When! Where! — nay, pri' thee now unfold it.

Cupid

'Gad — so I will; for faith I cannot hold it.
His mighty godship in a fiery flurry
Met me just now — confusion to his hurry!
I stopt his way, forsooth, and with a thwack,
He laid a thunderbolt across my back:
Bless me! I feel it now — my short ribs ache yet —
I vow'd revenge, and now by Styx I'll take it.
Miss Maia, in her chamber, after nine
Receives the thund'rer, in his robes divine.
I undermined it all; see, here's the letter —
Could dukes spell worse, whose tutors spell no better?
You know false spelling now is much the fashion —

Juno

Lend me your drops — Oh! I shall swoon with passion!

There is much broad comedy when Bacchus is
brought roistering in, and local and topical references that must have been salad to a smart London
audience.   In fact the whole thing is infinitely divert-
ing, witty, and bright and must have shown Chatter-

ton that he had a facility in light catchy verse as well as in the somber strains of a more enduring art.

"The Revenge" was submitted to Atterbury, proprietor of Marylebone Gardens. He accepted it and paid Chatterton five guineas for it,[1] the largest sum the boy ever received for any work and the only instance when his wage approximated his labor. The piece was acted at the gardens, but not until some months after its acceptance, other matters probably intervening.

Encouraged by the success of "The Revenge," he now undertook another comedy, this time in prose, "The Woman of Spirit," but did not complete it. He had, meantime, changed his lodging from the plasterer's at Shoreditch to Brooke Street, Holborn, No. 39, where he rented a front room in the attic of Mrs. Frederick Angell, a dressmaker. He had various reasons for making the change, but the strongest was that he saw the rapid decline of his prospects in the ruin of his friends, and his pride would not let him reveal to his relatives how straightened were his circumstances and how closely he must economize to avoid imminent disaster. They might write of it to his mother. The five guineas he had of Atterbury merely sufficed to tide him over for two or three weeks and meantime next to nothing was coming in. From the first his pay had been wretched.

[1] According to a note by one of Chatterton's editors the manuscript of this work was subsequently sold for 150 pounds.

For sixteen songs that Hamilton bought of him for the *Town and Country Magazine* he had received but 10 shillings 6 pence; for the long satirical poem of the "Consuliad" Fell paid him 10 shillings 6 pence; paragraphs in the *Town and Country* brought 2 shillings; a variety of work in the *Middlesex Journal*, for May, including the political essays I have described and quoted from, earned only 1 pound, 11 shillings, 6 pence. His entire earnings for the month of May (on the whole his most prosperous month) were only 4 pounds, 15 shillings, 9 pence. In June he earned 3 pounds, 13 shillings, 6 pence in essays and elegies on Beckford's death, but he published at his own expense a more elaborate elegy on his friend and this ate into his little capital.

And yet enough money was owing him at this time to support him in comfort, despite the difficulties created by the resurgence of feudalism; Hamilton of the *Town and Country*, for instance, had accepted of him manuscripts that he continued to publish for more than a year. But the boy's pride would not let him complain of these conditions. It was his old story, the old familiar tryanny of the strong upon the weak. They were men, he was a boy, and they took full advantage of the superior position.

Hence for the majority of the writings that with such infinite toil he produced in those lonely months in London he received nothing; for the rest he had pittances, the price of a slender meal, may be a few shillings at the most.

Among the works that Hamilton shortly had of him was another flight of song from Rowley. The glossary from Bristol had arrived and in the quiet attic in Brooke Street Rowley lifted up his voice again and sang at his sweetest and to this effect:

AN EXCELENTE BALADE OF CHARITIE:

as wroten bie the gode prieste
Thomas Rowleie, 1464

[1] In Virgo now the sultry sun did sheene,
   And hot upon the meads did cast his ray;
   The apple reddened from its paly green,
   And the soft pear did bend the leafy spray;
   The pied chelandry[2] sang the live long day;
   'Twas now the pride, the manhood of the year,
And eke the ground was decked in its most deft aumere.[3]

   The sun was gleaming in the midst of day,
   Dead-still the air, and eke the welkin blue,
   When from the sea arose in drear array
   A heap of clouds of sable sullen hue,
   The which full fast unto the woodland drew,
   Hiding at once the red sun's festive face,
And the black tempest swelled, and gathered up apace.

   Beneath a holm,[4] fast by a pathway side,
   Which did unto Saint Godwin's convent lead,

---

[1] The text as here given is modernized, but I fear indifferently. As so often before noted in these pages only the original can show Chatterton's real art.   [2] goldfinch.   [3] mantle.   [4] holly tree.

A hapless pilgrim moaning did abide.
Poor in his view, ungentle in his weed,
Long brimful of the miseries of need,
Where from the hailstorm could the beggar fly?
He had no houses there, nor any convent nigh.

Look in his gloomy face, his sprite there scan;
How woe-begone, how withered, dwindled, dead!
Haste to thy church-glebe-house, thou wretched man!
Haste to thy shroud, thine only sleeping bed.
Cold as the clay that will rest on thy head
Are Charity and Love among high elves;
For knights and barons live for pleasure and themselves.

The gathered storm is ripe; the big drops fall,
The sun-burnt meadows smoke, and drink the rain;
The coming ghastness doth the kine appal,
And the full flocks are driving o'er the plain;
Dashed from the clouds, the waters rise again;
The welkin opes, the yellow lightning flies,
And the hot fiery steam in the wide flashings dies.

List! now the thunder's startling noisy sound
Moves slowly on, and then full-swollen clangs,
Shakes the high spire, and lost, expended, drowned,
Still on the affrighted ear of terror hangs.
The winds are up; the lofty elmtree swangs:
Again the lightning, and the thunder pours,
And the full clouds are burst at once in torrent showers.

Spurring his palfrey o'er the watery plain,
The Abbot of Saint Godwin's convent came;
His chapournette[1] was all a-drench with rain,
His pointed girdle met with mickle stain;

[1] A small round hat.

He backwards told his beadroll at the same;[1]
The storm increasing then he drew aside
With the poor alms-craver near to the holm to bide.

His cope was all of Lincoln cloth so fine,
With a gold button fastened near his chin,
His autremete[2] was edged with golden twine,
And his shoe's peak a noble's might have been;
Full well it showed he thought great cost no sin.
The trammels of his palfrey pleased his sight,
For the horse-milliner his head with roses dight.

"An alms, sir priest!" the drooping pilgrim said,
"Oh! let me wait within your convent-door
Till the sun shineth high above our head,
And the loud tempest of the air is o'er.
Helpless and old am I, alas! and poor.
No house, no friend, no money in my pouch,
All that I call my own is this my silver crouche." [3]

"Varlet!" replied the abbot, "cease your din;
This is no season alms and prayers to give;
My porter never lets a faitour[4] in;
None touch my ring who not in honor live."
And now the sun with the black clouds did strive,
And shot upon the ground his glaring ray;
The abbot spurred his steed, and eftsoon rode away.

Once more the sky was black, the thunder rolled.
Fast running o'er the plain a priest was seen.
Not dight full proud, nor buttoned up in gold,
His cope and jape were grey, and eke were clean;

---

[1] Chatterton explained this in his own notes as a form of cursing
[2] A loose white robe.   [3] cross.   [4] beggar.

A limitor[1] he was of order seen;
And from the pathway then aside turned he,
Where the poor beggar lay beneath the holmen tree.

"An alms, sir priest!" the drooping pilgrim said,
"For sweet Saint Mary and your order's sake."
The limitor then loosened his pouch-thread,
And did thereout a groat of silver take:
The needy pilgrim did for gladness shake.
"Here, take this silver, it may ease thy care,
We are God's stewards all, naught of our own we bear.

"But ah! unhappy pilgrim, learn of me:
Scarce any give a rentroll to their lord;
Here, take my semicope, thou'rt bare, I see,
'Tis thine; the saints will give me my reward."
He left the pilgrim and his way aborde.
Virgin and holy saints, who sit in gloure,
Or give the mighty will, or give the good man power!

This eloquent cry of a soul that had felt the pinch of the world's inhumanity and learned the rarity of human charity, Hamilton, for some reason, rejected; the *Town and Country Magazine* had published scores of less effective works from the same pen.

He continued to write home the bravest letters, full of courage and cheering news and to lay out a part of his small earnings in presents for the three persons to whom his affections clung so steadfastly that now no one can unmoved read of their expression. He received his five guineas from Atterbury

[1] A licensed begging friar.

on July 6 and went at once to buy presents for Bristol. He knew quite well that he was facing sore trouble and very likely want. With a great-hearted generosity for which he has never had credit, he utterly disregarded his own possible needs to give pleasure to others. On July 8 he wrote to his mother as follows:

"DEAR MOTHER, — I send you in the box, six cups and saucers with two basins for my sister. If a china teapot and creampot is in your opinion, necessary, I will send them; but I am informed they are unfashionable, and that the red china, which you are provided with, is more in use. A cargo of patterns for yourself, with a snuffbox, right French, and very curious in my opinion.

Two fans — the silver one is more grave than the other, which would suit my sister best. But that I leave to you both. Some British herb snuff, in the box; be careful how you open it. (This I omit lest it injure the other matters.) Some British herb tobacco for my grandmother; some trifles for Thorne. Be assured whenever I have the power, my will won't be wanting to testify that I remember you.

Yours,
T. CHATTERTON.

N. B. — I shall forestall your intended journey, and pop down upon you at Christmas.

I could have wished you had sent my red pocket-book, as 'tis very material.

I bought two very curious twisted pipes for my grandmother; but both breaking, I was afraid to buy others lest they should break in the box; and being loose, injure the china. . . .

Direct for me at Mrs. Angell's, Sackmaker, Brook-street, Holborn.

To Mary he wrote:

DEAR SISTER, — I have sent you some china and a fan. You have your choice of two. I am surprised that you chose purple and gold. I went into the shop to buy it; but it is the most disagreeable colour I ever saw — dead, lifeless, and inelegant. Purple and pink, or lemon and pink, are more genteel and lively. Your answer in this affair will oblige me. Be assured, that I shall ever make your wants my wants; and stretch to the utmost to serve you. Remember me to Miss Sandford, Miss Rumsey, Miss Singer, &c.

As to the songs, I have waited this week for them, and have not had time to copy one perfectly; when the season's over, you will have 'em all in print. I had pieces last month in the following magazines:

Gospel Magazine.

Town and Country, viz:

> "Maria Friendless"
> "False Step"
> "Hunter of Oddities"
> "To Miss Bush," &c.

Court and City, London, Political Register, &c.

The *Christian Magazine,* as they are not to be had perfect, are not worth buying.

I remain, yours,
T. CHATTERTON.

July 11, 1770.

I am now about an Oratorio, which, when finished, will purchase you a gown. You may be certain of seeing me before the 1st January, 1771. — The clearance is immaterial. — My mother may expect more patterns. — Almost all the next *Town and Country Magazine* is mine. I have an universal acquaintance; my company is courted everywhere; and, could I humble myself to go into a comptor, could have had twenty places before now; — but I must be among the great; state matters suit me better than commercial. The ladies are not out of my acquaintance. I have a deal of business now, and must therefore bid you adieu. You will have a longer letter from me soon — and more to the purpose.

Yours,

T. C.

20th July, 1770.

July drifted by in a fierce dogged struggle against bare necessity. He was like a land-bird blown out to sea and struggling with almost exhausted wings against the certain fate of the waves. August came, the great town was very dull, the magazines were inert, the powerful and rich and happy all gone away, the tired drudge of Brooke Street fighting on alone. Casting about for some hope when his fortunes began to go awry he had thought of a position as surgeon's mate on a ship to Africa. In these deepening troubles the idea recurred to him. He had studied medicine and probably knew as much of it as many practising physicians of that age. In one of his letters to his mother he had given such advice for the treatment of a sick friend of the family as showed that he could put his studies to practical use. To be surgeon's mate on an African ship in those days required no more abstruse medical knowledge than the correct doses of a few standard drugs

and how to set a broken limb. Chatterton felt
that he possessed so much. But to secure the position it was needful that he should have an endorsement, and he turned to his old friend Barrett of
Bristol. Writing to Catcott August 12, after some
paragraphs of apparently light-hearted raillery and
comments of no moment, through which disguise it
is quite possible to see the tortured soul, he brings on
at the last, with an obviously assumed unconcern, the
plea that prompted the letter:

"I intend going abroad as a surgeon. Mr. Barrett has it in
his power to assist me greatly, by his giving me a physical character. I hope he will. I trouble you with a copy of an Essay I
intend publishing," etc.

He wrote also to Barrett himself, preferring the
same request. About August 18 he had Barrett's
answer. It consisted of a cold refusal.[1]

At Mrs. Angell's he had the attic, square and, for
an attic, rather large. It had dormer latticed windows that looked toward the street. In front of the
windows were a gutter and a low parapet wall, but
with an effort it was possible for one to look down
upon the passing throngs below. The roof every-

[1] Even this gratuitous cruelty has not lacked its defenders. There was
practically no science of medicine in those days. Scores of men that knew
far less about drugs than Chatterton knew were afloat as surgeon's mates.
When Smollett went to sea in that capacity he probably was not so well
equipped for the post as Chatterton would have been.

where was so low that in the highest place the boy could hardly stand erect with his hat on. It sloped gradually from the ridge-pole to the windows, which admitted the morning sunlight when any might be, and from which there was a view of St. Paul's Cathedral dome. Over it morning after morning he saw the sun rise as he sat toiling at his tasks, and again the afternoon come and gild it, the great curves look ruddy, the last glow fade slowly away as the day died. So much it had meant to him in his dreams! This was the very sign of the wonderful London that back in Bristol, where his mother and sister were, he had so often pictured to himself. About that great dome were the shops of the book-sellers that were to have made him famous and brought for him the money to make the household happy. His works were to have been sold about that place, he had always thought so, and now there were only cold looks and shut doors. It was all so different; so different from those first good days, even. The publishers had welcomed him then, and had wanted him to write more and more, and now no one seemed to care for anything he wrote. Hamilton, of the *Town and Country*, had been glad to print "Elinoure and Juga," and now he rejected that "Excelente Balade of Charitie," that the boy knew was worth a dozen of the other. And the battlefield was quite deserted and silent; only a few weeks ago he was a leader among men, and now he was forgotten, the army he had fought with beaten and dispersed. There was the reward of his labor justly due him, and to every intimation that he would like to have the debt paid he received nothing but black looks and frigid answers. The world had been against him from the first. He had been beaten for reading and dreaming about the tomb of Canynge, when he meant no harm to any one, but only wanted to be alone with his thoughts and his tears. He had been beaten for writing poetry, and how could that hurt any one or be a crime? Only because he was a boy and poor and obscure he had been despised and insulted by the man to whom he had turned for help. And now the world of men, so much bigger and stronger than he, was cheating him of the earnings of his toil because he was a boy, merely a boy. Was there any place in the world for the weak and the unhappy? What was all mankind organized for but for the strong to prey upon the weak and to trample to success over broken hearts? And it was all so different from what he had imagined. Where were all his bright dreams now? And what should he say to his mother that had expected such glorious achievement from him? And there was the dome, the symbol of his hope, and every morning it shone upon him just as it had shone when the world was bright and his future so alluring. And of all that what remained?

One thing was certain, the little household at Bristol must know nothing about his distress. So he set himself to compose a letter in his old vein of raillery and good spirits. He jested as usual about the people he had met and the things he had seen, and told them a story — very doubtful — about an adventure of his own in a graveyard where he said he had accidentally fallen into a new-made grave, but had found the sexton under him and emerged with laughter. But all would not do; the gaiety was too forced to deceive the ready clairvoyance of a mother. Mrs. Chatterton saw from this letter that something was wrong, that the boy was trying to conceal something from her, and from that time she was distressed about him. She called in Mrs. Edkins to read to her the letter and tell her fears about it, and the two wept over the reading. It was all gay and brave and light-hearted, but in it there was a note of forced laughter more terrifying than despair.

And yet in his misery he fronted the world with unshaken courage and a heart as tender as brave. A part of the last money he received he had devoted to the happiness and comfort of the little household at Bristol, and now, wretched as he was, he heard the appeals of others in trouble like his own. His last little pocket-book, recently acquired by the Bristol Museum, tells the story entered in his neat hand and with his methodical care. There was owing to him, it shows, £10, 17s. 6d. for the articles that he had sent to the magazines. And there are two little entries that lay bare his very soul. "Lent 2s." and "Lent 1s. 6d." There was no distress that could chill the boundless generosity of that spirit.

At last his money was all gone; for some days he had been starving. His wan, haggard face and feverish anxiety began to attract attention. At the corner of Brooke Street and Holborn, a short distance from Mrs. Angell's, one Cross, a kindly man, kept an apothecary shop. Chatterton had made some acquaintance with him and it had fared with him as with all other capable minds that knew the boy; the charm of brilliant conversation, the poise, the frank manner, and the marvelous eyes had won him with the rest. He suspected that all was not well with his young friend and cautiously invited him to dine. Chatterton declined; but the invitation being renewed on several occasions as Cross observed the boy passing in the street, at last it was accepted and Cross was rather shocked to see how voraciously his guest ate. Mrs. Angell, too, a motherly good soul, had an eye on him. She was confident that for two days together he had eaten nothing, and waylaying him on the stairs urged him to share her meal. But something in the well-meant invitation went awry and struck up that overweening pride. He curtly refused and assured her he was not hungry.

This was on August 24, 1770, when he was seventeen years and nine months old. Some time before he had obtained a little arsenic, some persons have supposed of Cross on the plea that he wished to poison the rats in his chamber. On this evening he retired as usual to his room. They heard him walking about there a little, but so he did often. Through what solemn agony he passed in those hours is only to be surmised. He opened his little trunk and took from it manuscript after manuscript and tore each into minute fragments, the fruits of his labor, the dear children of his thoughts that he had reared in his loneliness and pain, the hurt father turning upon and rending all. And that done, he mixed his arsenic with water and drank it, and throwing himself upon his little bed, he died.

In the morning they broke open his door and found him there, dead in the ruins of so much hope. The world of London roared on and never knew how great a soul it had trampled under its careless heel. Of him lying dead in his attic chamber a scant half-dozen strangers took heed. The coroner came and held a perfunctory inquest, making no notes and in haste to be gone; Mrs. Angell, her husband, and a neighbor testified, the verdict of suicide was reached, the permit issued, the coroner went about his business. The men from the parish workhouse came with a rude coffin and bore off the poor little body,

The House where Chatterton Died, No. 39 Brooke Street, London.
(From an old print in the possession of the Bristol Museum.)

and that night it went to the potter's field of the Shoe Lane workhouse. Nobody took note of the event; the newspapers printed no word of it, Wilkes on the Continent, Fell and Edmunds in prison, heard nothing about it; and on the registry of St. Andrews, Holborn,[1] in which parish lay Brooke Street and Shoe Lane, the rare melodist thus made mute was entered as "William Chatterton."

Yet at that moment Dr. Fry, of Oxford, the one man in all England that had perceived the surpassing wonder of the Rowley poems, whether true or false, was preparing a journey to Bristol to find this marvelous young man and assist him if he should need help. And yet at that moment the miserly Hamilton owed him several pounds for work he had accepted and that he continued to publish for more than a year.

But perhaps his last resting place may not have been in the lost promiscuity of the potter's field; the

[1] Remarkable coincidences attend this strange story. The rector of St. Andrews, Holborn, in which parish Brooke Street is situated, was Chatterton's old acquaintance and adversary at Bristol, the Rev. Dr. Broughton, and it was in the registry of his church that the erroneous name was entered in noting the burial. Broughton was at St. Andrews all the time that Chatterton lived in Brooke Street, but though Chatterton knew this very well he made no effort to see the former Bristolian.

While he was still in Lambert's office Chatterton seems to have become deeply impressed with the story of Richard Savage, the unfortunate poet. In several of the acknowledged poems are sympathetic references to Savage, whose joyless life and melancholy fate resembled his own. Now Savage was born in Brooke Street where Chatterton died, and died in Bristol where Chatterton was born.

veil of that restless spirit may have come home to the shadow of the church he loved, and the churchyard where as a little boy he used to run about holding the sexton's fingers. Some reasons exist to believe that his mother, most desirous that her son might be buried in consecrated ground, sent word to a relative of hers in London, a carpenter, who reclaimed the body and sent it in a box to Bristol. Over it, in the upper part of her house, the mother held a secret vigil, showing it to but one friend, and at night Phillips, the sexton, now an old man and near his own death, took the little form and buried it by stealth in the yard of St. Mary's. The very spot is pointed out: it is "to the south of the church on the right hand side of the lime-tree in the middle paved walk in Redcliffe church-yard," where his father and mother and sister lie. In the morning the shadow of St. Mary Redcliffe falls upon it and at noon the clear sunlight. A strange hush seems always to dwell in that churchyard, deep and unending peace is there in the heart of the great city; the thick trees shut out the world, all day falls scarcely a footstep, and sitting there I have heard the strains of the organ playing Mendelssohn's "Consolation" as if from a great way off.

VII

THE WORLD'S VERDICT

So the wonderful voice passed to silence, but the songs it had sung had only begun to live. At first the boy's death made no ripple on the current of passing events. If Barrett and Catcott, who had so much profited by their young friend, were grieved by his loss, they made no record of their feelings. The first tribute of which we have record is an elegy that Chatterton's friend, Thomas Cary, published in the *Town and Country Magazine* for October of that year. It was full of genuine feeling; Chatterton must have meant much to Cary, judging by his affectionate and unstudied phrases. It was six months before there was further reference to the story. Dr. Fry, of Oxford, had made his journey to Bristol and collected some fragments of the Rowley poems. Perhaps through his agency they had been brought to the attention of Oliver Goldsmith. At a dinner of the Royal Academy, April 23, 1771, Goldsmith announced to the company, in which were Dr. Johnson and all the distinguished literary men of London, that at Bristol had been discovered a store of ancient poems, most wonderful and beautiful; that he had examined some of them and believed them to be genuine. Among the diners was Horace Walpole. He pricked up his ears when he heard this announcement and, of course, did not fail to tell the company that he knew all about the poems and the person that had discovered them, and he related the verdict of Gray and Mason. Goldsmith still protested his faith in Rowley, and the talk going on it came out presently from Goldsmith's own lips that the discoverer of Rowley had been in London and had killed himself there. So much the good Goldsmith had been at pains to discover.

This introduction to the attention of the literary world of London naturally bore fruit in inquiries about the poems and the boy that said he had found them. Interested persons began to visit and write to Bristol, asking about these matters. The Rowley manuscripts began to be sought for. Most of them were in the hands of Catcott, and this person finally conceiving that there might be commercial value in productions that he had regarded as mere curiosities, executed a stroke of business for himself by purchasing from Mrs. Chatterton such of the boy's manuscripts as she possessed. As he gave her five guineas for these papers and subsequently sold them to a London publisher for fifty pounds the profit would seem to have been fair. The inquiries steadily increased;

requests for permission to copy the manuscripts in the hands of Barrett and Catcott were frequently made. In three years after Chatterton's death the Earl of Lichfield possessed a fairly good collection of these copies, and literary men frequently debated of their genuineness. In 1776 Johnson and Boswell joined the pilgrims to Bristol, and Johnson made some investigation of the evidences for Rowley, which Catcott and Barrett, and indeed all Bristol, implicitly believed in. Johnson quickly saw that Catcott was a foolish person and that the poems were of modern manufacture; but in the end, although the acknowledgment overturned his favorite theory that no untrained mind can notably achieve, he owned the boy's amazing genius. "This is the most extraordinary young man that has encountered my knowledge," he said; "it is wonderful how the whelp has written such things."

In 1777 the constantly growing interest in the poems had reached a point where publication was demanded, and a small edition of Rowley, made up from the Barrett and Catcott manuscripts, was printed in London by Tyrwhitt. This was reissued the next year with some additional matter. Four years later appeared another and much fuller volume, and in 1794 the pretentious Cambridge edition, edited by Lancelot Sharpe. For reasons to be dealt with hereafter the poems had become the first subject of concern in the learned world. And yet while scholars were studying Chatterton's works and kind-hearted men and women were grieving over his fate, Catcott and Barrett went their way unaffected. From Catcott, indeed, not much was to be expected at any time except froth and folly, but what are we to make of the strange silence of Barrett? He knew for how much of his "History and Antiquities" he was indebted to this boy; he knew that he himself had assisted in the Burgum pedigree and the Walpole correspondence, both presently the subject of controversy or comment; he knew that he had been Chatterton's closest and most intimate acquaintance; he knew how much he had been confidant and counselor to that sorely-tried spirit. He knew, too, how much the pretended antiques furnished by Chatterton had differed from the genuine documents supplied by Morgan, and knew how in the boy's last extremity he had withheld the helping hand that would have saved that extraordinary life. But whatever secrets that frigid bosom held went with him to the grave. He made no sign about them. He was living in Bristol when Chatterton's mother and sister were in the utmost distress and poverty; he never manifested the slightest interest in them. His little round of life lay in his book; his only concern was to secure for himself unclouded the glory of that marvelous achievement, and he was obviously annoyed that people should think about Chatterton when they might be thinking about Barrett. In a last chapter, devoted to biographical notices of eminent sons of Bristol, he had much to say of Rowley, but of Chatterton, only a cold and incidental line about "T. Chatterton, the producer of Rowley and his poems to the world," and a harsh comment about his "horrible end" and "libertine principles."[1]

But elsewhere, when it was too late, an effort was made to balance the world's account with this great spirit. Two kind-hearted men, of Bristol birth, Robert Southey, the poet, and Joseph Cottle, were especially moved by the story and cast about to be of some service to the family. Mrs. Chatterton had died in 1791. Mary had been married and widowed, and with her children was living in dire poverty, visited and somewhat relieved by Hannah More, who was also of Bristol, and from the natural goodness of her heart benevolently interested in the Chattertons. Southey and Cottle were not rich, but they did what they could; they edited and published in 1803 the best edition of Chatterton's works that had so far appeared, and they gave the entire proceeds to Mary. She died in 1804, leaving a daughter, who was supported by the income money

[1] It should not be inferred that this phrase coming from such a source has any bearing on the question of Chatterton's character. In those days all persons that doubted the divine right of kings or questioned the inerrancy of the scriptures were likely to be subjected to such comment.

from the Southey and Cottle edition until her death in 1807. She was the last of the Chattertons.

A great and invaluable part of our knowledge of the records of Thomas Chatterton's life we owe to an incident in no way connected with it, and to the intrusion of one of the most singular figures in English literature. On the night of April 7, 1779, one Hackman, a clergyman whose career had also included service as an officer in the 66th regiment of the British Army, startled London by shooting a popular actress named Miss Ray as she was leaving Covent Garden Theater. He had long been madly in love with her and had made violent proposals of marriage. It appears that when she refused him he determined to kill himself in her presence, but unluckily changed his intention and shot her instead. The event was a nine days' sensation in London and suggested to the Rev. Sir Herbert Croft the writing of a very strange book called "Love and Madness," which consisted of pretended letters of Hackman to Miss Ray and her replies. This pseudo-correspondence dealt with love, lovers, and suicide, with Goethe and the "Sorrows of Werther," and finally at some length with the story of Chatterton. The inclusion was both repulsive and grotesque, for Chatterton was never in love and assuredly he was not insane, but we need not quarrel with the motives that produced results of so much importance. To prepare himself to deal with the Chatterton story Croft made laborious, painstaking investigations. He went out to Shoreditch and interviewed Mrs. Ballance and the honest plasterer and his family. He talked with the young man that had been Chatterton's roommate. He examined them in detail, like a prosecuting attorney. He went to Brooke Street and tried to find Mrs. Angell. He hunted up the coroner that had held the inquest. He discovered and preserved some of Chatterton's best letters. He went to Bristol and saw Mrs. Chatterton and others. He had a mind insatiable of details and a faculty for persistent inquiry that in our day would have made him a priceless reporter for a newspaper. He went over all the ground, asking innumerable questions and making voluminous notes, and as most of the persons that had known Chatterton were still living, "Love and Madness" became the great storehouse of information about the last days of the unfortunate boy. He had, to tell the truth, no great sympathy with the case, nor with Chatterton's art, but his unsympathetic attitude made his investigations all the better for us. From all the persons he interviewed, from the dwellers in Shoreditch and in Brooke Street, from Cross the apothecary, and the rest, the testimony he obtained was uniformly of the boy's blameless life, prodigious industry, and goodness of heart.

Not a word indicated loose conduct, not a suggestion
reflected on his character. And of his endowment,
Croft, his inquiries finished, declared that "no such
human being, at any period of life, has ever been
known or possibly ever will be known." This
unequivocal testimony by one that knew more about
Chatterton's real life than any other writer has known,
has been overlooked by all but one of Chatterton's
biographers. It could hardly be more explicit or
convincing. Whoever will take the trouble now to
examine the products of this unaccountable mind,
the incomprehensible record of his labors, the
achievements in so many directions, the versatility
and power, will agree with me that Croft's verdict
was not extravagant. All in all this was certainly
the most wonderful intellect that the English-speaking race has ever produced with the one exception of
Shakespeare, and the boy that possessed it was
driven by starvation to kill himself before he was
eighteen years old.

Several biographical sketches of Chatterton had
appeared in connection with editions of his works or
independently, but the first extensive and formal
life was published in 1837 by John Dix. Unluckily
it mixed imaginary details with the attested gatherings of Croft and others until few puzzles are more
trying than to tell where Dix's facts left off and his
fancies began. He managed to increase the biog-

rapher's difficulties in other ways, for not only have his imaginings been incorporated with the texture of the narrative, but they have had ingenious embroidery from other hands. But there is scarcely a story in English history that has been more befuddled. Dix raised the question of Chatterton's burial place by printing (for the first time) in an appendix the statement of George Cumberland (to which I am coming shortly), concerning his investigations in Bristol in 1808. No effort was made by Dix to corroborate this statement, although he spent some time in Bristol where there was at least one person that might have made a good witness.

Nothing could now be of keener concern to those that feel an interest in this friendless boy than to know the truth about this matter, but the time has long gone by when the truth could be ascertained. The story of the midnight burial is thoroughly disbelieved in Bristol, and has been discredited by most writers about Chatterton, although the incredulity of the writers is of no moment since the bulk of such writing has been done to suit prejudice or preconceived theory and without much regard to the testimony. Between inherent improbability and direct statement the balance seems even. There was one person in Bristol, aside from the Chattertons, that would be likely to know of the burial, if there had been such a thing. That Mrs. Edkins, their lifelong and devoted friend, Chatterton's companion in his trips among the beggars, Mrs. Chatterton's close associate, would know if anybody knew. Accordingly, in 1853, the handful of students that followed the Chatterton story was startled by a statement from Mr. Joseph Cottle, who, as we have seen, was one of Chatterton's editors, declaring that Mrs. Edkins had verified the whole story. Curiously enough the verification had not been given to him but to the same George Cumberland that Dix had quoted, and Cumberland had transmitted it to Cottle. According to Cottle Mrs. Edkins had said: "Mrs. Chatterton was passionately fond of her darling and only son, Thomas; and, when she heard he had destroyed himself, she immediately wrote to a relation of hers, a carpenter, urging him to send home his body in a coffin or box. The box was accordingly sent down to Bristol; and when I called on my friend, Mrs. Chatterton, to condole with her, she, as a very great secret, took me up-stairs and showed me the box; and removing the lid I saw the poor boy whilst his mother sobbed in silence. She told me that she should have him taken out in the middle of the night, and bury him in Redcliffe churchyard. Afterwards when I saw her she said she had managed it very well, so that none but the sexton and his assistant knew anything about it. This secrecy was necessary, as he could not be buried in consecrated ground."

This seemed conclusive enough on the face of it, but its credibility weakened on examination. The statement from Cumberland that Dix printed in his appendix gave a very different version of his conversation with Mrs. Edkins, and one that contained no reference to the box or the burial. But a Mrs. Stockwell, who had likewise been an intimate friend of Mrs. Chatterton's and one of her pupils, certainly told Cumberland that the boy was buried in Redcliffe and indicated the spot. She said Mrs. Chatterton had assured her in confidence of this and told her all about the arrival of the body and the burial by Phillips. She gave a circumstantial account, also, of a permission that Mrs. Chatterton had given to one Hutchinson to bury his child over her son's grave, and how much Mrs. Chatterton had subsequently regretted this. Some minor points in this narrative were subsequently corroborated, but the main fact remained undetermined. Mrs. Chatterton, her daughter, and the sexton had died before any one thought it worth while to investigate the matter; if the sexton performed the burial he never mentioned it to his family; and all chance of direct confirmation was lost. The question takes on a phase of still more painful interest because fifty years after Chatterton's death Shoe Lane workhouse was torn down to make room for Farringdon market and, with callous indifference, the bodies in the potter's field near by were dug up and carted away, no one knows whither. It is hard to think of the body of Thomas Chatterton thrown upon a rubbish heap. After spending much time in Bristol and weighing the scraps of evidence, guesses, and surmises obtainable from many sources, it seems to me clear that Mr. Cottle, who was very old when he wrote his statement, confused Mrs. Edkins with Mrs. Stockwell, and on Mrs. Stockwell's testimony, with the slight collateral facts Cumberland was able to obtain, rests all the story of the burial in Redcliffe churchyard. Edward Bell, who has written of Chatterton more intelligently than any other man except Professor Wilson, of Toronto, gives credence to the story and unfeignedly I wish that I could.

But in the meantime Rowley and Chatterton had shaken the literary world. The third edition of the poems had been printed in 1782, and on its issuing began the most extraordinary controversy in English literature, the most extraordinary, the least reasonable, and on the whole, the most humiliating. The last shot in that warfare was fired in 1857, and between the dates there had been more sound and fury over what signified nothing than can be paralleled in modern history.

The inspiration and pilot of the edition of 1782 was an unfortunate gentleman named Jeremiah Milles, who happened, by some grotesque freak of

fate, to be president of the Society of Antiquaries.
He was also D.D. and Dean of Exeter. He illumined
his editing with a long "Commentary" full of pretentious ignorance, in which, in his own phrase, he
"considered and defended" the antiquity of the
poems. It is not too much to say that the average
high school boy of Kansas or Oklahoma would blush
to display the Dean's crass ignorance about the
English language and its literature. Sad, indeed,
was the spectacle afforded; the whole futility of
English scholarship and the English University
seemed to be laid bare. This D.D. and President
of the Society of Antiquaries knew nothing of the
history of the English stage and drama, nothing of
the development of his language, nothing of medieval
life and customs. He did not know that discovery of
such a drama as "Aella" purporting to be of the
fifteenth century would be like discovery of a repeating rifle among the weapons of the Stone age. He
knew nothing about the history of English poetry; it
never occurred to him that the Rowley poems were
written in a highly developed melodic strain and that
melody had existed in English verse hardly two centuries. He knew nothing about Chaucer, nothing
about Lydgate, nothing about the intellectual state of
the Saxons, nothing about their history or manners,
and of Rowley, Turgot, Abbot John, Bishop This
and Bishop That, the long list of impossible Saxon

painters and all the rest he made one meal and was ready to swallow more. To his mind the Rowley poems were indubitable, and to crown his absurdities with a perfect climax he founded much of his argument upon internal evidence.

On the appearance of this wondrous document the lists were set and the coursing began. Malone and Tyrwhitt, the ablest scholars of their times, came out with powerful essays riddling Milles's arguments and showing a small part of the evidence of modern origin that in this day is obvious to practically every reader. In that day it had to be dragged out and laid in courses like stones for a house. Warton, of Oxford, author of a history of English poetry and an authority enormously overrated in his day, fought on the same side. This seemed a powerful phalanx; it was assaulted with a ponderous tome written by one Jacob Bryant and rejoicing in the name of "Bryant's Observations," in which all that Milles had said was enforced and with painstaking imbecility endless chapters of new argument were added. The magazines rang with this clishmaclaver; Rowleyans and Anti-Rowleyans ran tilts in every periodical. Dr. Fry, President of St. Johns, Oxford; Henry Dampier, Dean of Durham; Rayner Hickford, of Waxted; Lord Lyttleton and others, championed Rowley and supported Bryant and Milles. The number of learned men willing to exhibit themselves as knowing nothing of their own tongue or country steadily increased, no doubt for the refreshing by innocent merriment of future generations, and it seemed impossible to get the simplest facts of philological research established so that these unfortunate persons would recognize them. A new generation had come and gone before it began widely to be admitted that the Rowley poems had no other origin than in the fertile mind of Thomas Chatterton. Even so late as 1857, as I have said, a gentleman writing in "Notes and Queries" was still unconvinced and probably died unshaken in the Rowley faith, and in 1865 a writer in a London magazine argued that part, at least, of the Rowley romance was true.

The controversy may have been wholesome for English scholarship, inasmuch as it showed in a powerful manner how much less educated Englishmen knew of their own language than they knew of Latin and Greek; but it was ill for the fame of Thomas Chatterton. A short cut to prove that Rowley did write the poems was to show that Chatterton could not have written them; and for all that regard human nature as an alluring study it should be instructive to note that the favorite way to this proof was by asserting Chatterton to have been of dissolute habits and ordinary endowments. To this cheerful pursuit was much aid in the inevitable tendency of the British mind to moral-

ize for the benefit of the Young Person. Chatterton
was a boy, he held rationalistic beliefs, he told fibs,
he came to a bad end. Naturally, then, all must be
of one pattern; to admit that anything he did was
good was to endanger the morals of the Rising
Generation. Extraordinary are the chances of Geog-
raphy. If Chatterton had been born 240 miles
S. E. by E. of Bristol, no one would have thought
it essential that he be pilloried for the public good.
In England it has been different, and to this day
English writers, including many that have not read
and some that could not understand his works, have
not ceased to execrate him. Every line of his writings, every chance expression in his letters, every
unfavorable recollection of those that had not liked
or had envied him, has been exhumed and twisted
into a derogatory significance. Following the licentious manner of the times, he gave pen to much idle
and some objectionable matter, and all this has been
cited as proof that he was a libertine and depraved
person. The obvious fact that the enormous quantity of the work he turned out made it impossible
that he should have time for dissipation has been
conveniently neglected, with the testimony of his
London relatives as to the unvarying regularity of
his habits, and his own statement of his innate
abhorrence of the ways of vice. His innocent addresses to various young women of Bristol have been

tortured into meaning that he was a sad rake, his admiration for Wilkes and his bold attacks upon monarchy have been used to show his revolutionary and dangerous character, and over all have been spread the lurid colors of that word "forgery." The mere sound of it is enough. Forgery! Here was a "forger" and all the prejudices of a commercial age and race have pursued him up and down until the truth has been obscured to the general mind that this was a most wonderful intellect, that here were gifts as far beyond our understanding as Shakespeare's, that he was only a boy, and that the gross world trod out his light before it had more than flamed up once.

For some of this there is possible excuse in the heat and fury of controversy; but for the most of it, none. It is commonly assumed, among those that have never taken the trouble to investigate the story, that Chatterton put his fabrications upon the world, as Macpherson put his, for hire and salary; and the gratuitous assumption has done this unfortunate boy additional wrong. As a matter of fact, very few of the Rowley papers saw the light during their author's lifetime, and from all of his writings in imitation of the antique, of whatsoever kind, he can hardly have had so much as three pounds. The essence of forgery is an intent to defraud. Acres of paper covered with imitated handwritings would not constitute forgery unless they were used to gain something of value. When Chatterton died the mass of the Rowley poems were manuscripts in the hands of Barrett and Catcott. It was the publication of "Elinoure and Juga" and one or two others, and the incessant babbling of Catcott, that finally brought Rowley to the attention of antiquarians and thus to the notice of Dr. Fry, who was the first person to take any real interest in the matter. What, then, is more unjust than to class Thomas Chatterton with sordid impostors like Macpherson and Ireland? It was with no purpose of gain that he gave life to his dreams. But being born an artist, and his soul being wrapped in a certain subject, it was beyond his control that he should give expression to the things whereon he brooded and in the shape that answered to his visions. And this point has been consistently overlooked, that the Rowley romance was a thing apart from anything he did for money, that it represented only the artistic side of his nature, that in all human probability he could no more avoid the form of expression his work took than a painter can avoid putting into his painting the characteristics of his individual style. But monstrous injustice has been, from the time of his birth, the lot of this boy. No part of the strange story seems stranger than this, that dead now one hundred and thirty-seven years, the world still looks askance at him, and chiefly for the sake of the name applied to his work by the one man in England having the least right to condemn any one that did that particular thing. "If literary forgery were the capital offense," says Professor Wilson, "the same gallows should have sufficed for Walpole and Chatterton."

A few sympathetic souls bore heavily upon the Earl of Orford when the facts were revealed about the wonderful genius that had been sacrificed to indifference and neglect. Bitter comments were made in many places, and at last the noble earl took up his own defense. He had the bad taste to print a letter in which he thought to better his position by assailing the memory of the dead. He sneered at Chatterton's work, distorted what had happened between them, and set afloat or gave prominence to all the reports that were derogatory to his character. On other occasions he lied most outrageously about the affair. He denied having received the letters that he had answered, he accused Chatterton of betraying the cause in which he was enlisted, and his word as a nobleman bore such weight that men that should have known better were swayed out of a normal judgment. He had pretended that he was quite indifferent to Chatterton's cutting satires against him; he demonstrated that not only was he hurt by what the boy had written, but that he was capable of the ignoble revenge of maligning one no longer able to defend himself.

The truth is that Walpole is the sole authority for the idea that Chatterton was dissolute. You will find it advanced without proof, without reason, by his every biographer, but there is extant not one particle of evidence to support it and through all its reappearances it can be traced back, link by link, in an unfailing chain until we come to Walpole's letter of defense, and there we can put finger upon the source of all the slanders. Walpole asserts them; the first man echoes Walpole, the second man parrots the first, and so on from tome to tome the falsehood flies and gathers bulk. Walpole never saw Chatterton, had no knowledge of his ways or life or habits, never knew anybody that knew him, had no way to learn of these matters, and founded his adroitly worded accusation on a chance expression of Chatterton's in a letter to his sister: "I am this moment pierced through the heart by the black eye of a young lady," and the like innocent *jocoserie*. Upon this and upon nothing else. I have patiently searched out every line that has been written on this subject and have assured myself that Walpole's animadversions, as taken up and enlarged upon by those that desired for their own purposes to belittle Chatterton, were the one origin of all this most singular prejudice.

It was Walpole again that started the "forgery"

idea: "all the house of forgery are relations," he says, and proceeds to assert that Chatterton having succeeded in "forging" old poems would probably have gone on to forge notes of hand. The next edition of this humane remark appears in the Introduction to an early edition of Chatterton's Miscellanies in which the writer takes the cheerful view that Chatterton's early death was no great matter since if he had lived he would surely have been hanged. Of course, this is merely Walpole's suggestion clothed in other words. From that day to this the notion has somehow clung to the human intellect; Chatterton was a forger; all forgers are criminals and detestable creatures; therefore do not read Chatterton's works.

Again, without exception the biographers have taken as true the assertion that Chatterton wrote on both sides of the issue between king and people. Even Professor Wilson calls him for this a "venal young politician," and yet when this charge has been traced back from hand to hand we find it to have exactly the same basis as the other, that is to say Walpole's assertion and a mere phrase in one of Chatterton's letters to his sister. "He is a poor author, who cannot write on both sides," said the boy, and on these words have been based page upon page of moral disquisition and sage reproof. Walpole asserted that he had seen a manuscript signed

"Moderator," and written by Chatterton, in which the king's attitude towards the people of London was defended and praised. He did not say how he knew it was Chatterton's, nor where he saw it, nor when, nor who had it at the time, nor what became of it afterward. No one else has ever seen it, nor heard of anybody that had heard of anybody that had seen it. Nobody knows where it is now. But on the strength of such testimony the boy's character has been assailed.[1]

---

[1] Here I feel impelled to give an illustration of the ease and fluency with which "Chatterton Incidents" have been supplied.

"Three days before his death, when walking with a friend in St. Pancras churchyard, reading the epitaphs, he was so deep in thought as he walked on, that not perceiving a grave which was just dug, he fell into it: his friend, observing his situation, came to his assistance, and as he helped him out, told him in a jocular manner, he was happy in beholding the resurrection of genius. Poor Chatterton smiled, and taking his companion by the arm, replied, 'My dear friend, I feel the sting of a speedy dissolution. I have been at war with the grave for some time, and find it not so easy to vanquish as I imagined; we can find an asylum from every creditor but that.'"

For this engaging specimen of fictional art we are indebted to Dix (Life of Chatterton, p. 290). It is pure invention. In the last letter to his mother Chatterton wrote in a merry strain of falling into a grave upon the sexton at work therein and bouncing out laughingly. Upon this slight foundation and none other Dix reared the airy structure of his incident, not hesitating to supply the conversation or any other accessory. Three days before Chatterton's death he was not wandering with a friend in St. Pancras churchyard, but struggling gaunt-eyed and famished in his little garret. But his entire life has been maimed and distorted for us by the like imaginings of the early biographers, Gregory, Chalmers, Dix and the rest, each incorporating a previous fantasy and adding something of his own. Now, why should all these writers feel at liberty to imagine the details of a life about which they knew nothing?

It had been in the power of Horace Walpole to give Chatterton's works to the world and to save the life of one of the greatest geniuses that ever lived in any age or country, and his comment upon his conduct in that affair was that "all the house of forgery are relations." He had himself been guilty of a far worse offense in that same line, and yet the accusations that he had the effrontery to make have outweighed the facts and done more to pervert the truth about Thomas Chatterton than any other cause. He was rich, powerful, titled, one of the great men of his day, and he set his wits to undermine the character of the charity school boy that he had repulsed and unjustly treated, whose life he had embittered and of whose death he was not morally blameless.

Thus year after year Thomas Chatterton has been brought by the bailiffs of British morals to be judged of his offense, tried by the application of such standards as would befit one indicted for check-raising or counterfeiting, and unanimously condemned. For generations it seemed as if time would not ameliorate nor all the extenuating facts weigh against the sentence. To this day as often as he is mentioned he is regularly branded as the "Literary Forger." "It is such a dirty crime," says one of Charles Reade's characters, accused of forgery, and speaks a true word. It is like leprosy. Neither the literary nor

the moral reputation of this boy has been able to
stand against it. Shall there be anything good in
a forger?

But suppose we see how this matter stands.
Thomas Chatterton, aged fifteen, dreamer of dreams
and assuredly born out of his true time, clothed his
magnificent poetry in an antique dress and pretended that it had been written three hundred years
before, and this he did, not for mercenary purposes,
not for any profit he might secure, nor, very probably, with any consciousness of deceit, but from
some vague instinct of the requirements of an artistic
setting. Macpherson, a mature man, manufactured
his spurious Ossian stuff that he might with it swindle
confiding historical societies and impose upon publishers. It is a strange fact that in the literature of
this subject the offense of the man Macpherson
appears trivial compared with the misdoing of the
lonely charity school boy. No one now cares to castigate Macpherson; no one now issues books and
writes articles to gibbet him as an awful warning to
the young. The whole weight of abhorrence for literary forging is reserved for the boy; the man goes free.

Or take other illustrations. "Who wrote
Otranto?" asks Chatterton in one of his satirical
poems. He might well ask. When Walpole issued
his novel the "Castle of Otranto" he palmed it
upon an unsuspecting world as a translation of an

old Italian manuscript he had found, and for a
long time that dull hoax deceived everybody.
Yet no one now drags Horace Walpole to be
judged at the bar of public opinion; no one calls
the Earl of Orford "Literary Forger."   Mere feigning about the origin of a manuscript has never (in
other cases) been accounted a great matter.   It has
been done innumerable times without imping-
ing upon the sensitive nerves of professional
moralists.   Many an honored or respectable writer
of fiction from Scott to Stevenson has done it, often
concealing his own name and share in the performance, and no one has been mortally offended.   This
boy alone has been singled out for punishment.

In spite of all, the flame he lighted has burned on
steadily, year by year, his fame and the recognition
of his influence have grown among his own gild.
The poets knew at once that wonderful voice and
gave heed to a new and supernal message.   Coleridge
studied Chatterton attentively and repaid part of
what he learned in one of the most beautiful poems
in the language.   Blake yearned over him; Shelley [1]
understood and loved a spirit so much akin to his
own; Keats sat at his feet, dedicated "Endymion"
to his memory, and took from his works one
of the most celebrated and beautiful of his pic-

[1] Do but compare carefully the "Hymn of Apollo" with the stanzas from
"Aella" that are given on p. 145.

tures;[1] Wordsworth knew what the voice meant and paid it the tribute of his tears and of a deathless sonnet; Robert Buchanan sang again and again in his honor; Rossetti brought wreath after wreath for his unknown shrine. Of all the poets that have sung in English this is most truly the poet for poets; of all the poets that have sung in English, Shakespeare alone excepted, this has had upon what is distinctively the modern structure of the art the most stimulating influence; and of all the poets that have sung in English, Shakespeare alone excepted, this had the greatest gifts and surest inspiration.

We shall see what Chatterton did for English poetry if we compare what it was before him with what it became afterward; then the seeds of much of the splendid modern growth appear in his poems, not elsewhere. Taking a large view of modern poetry as an art, and tracing back its basic principles — designed melody of expression, designed use of color and form, the spirit of intimate and loving communion with nature, song that aims to transfer a feeling, not to express a sentiment nor to embody a syllogism — the evolution of all these things may be traced back from Swinburne to Tennyson, from Tennyson to Shelley and Keats, from Shelley and Keats to Coleridge and Wordsworth, from poet to

[1] Not only this, but many a line in "Endymion" and the Odes was obviously inspired by lines in "Aella" and in Chatterton's songs.

poet, from generation to generation, back to the charity school boy of Bristol, but no farther.

From its long descent into the desert places that began after Milton, English poetry was certain to return, else it would have perished of inanition. On the starveling desert fare and laden with the rubbish of metaphysics and "thought," it lost all trace of the beauty and freshness of its youth. From the beginning of Dryden to the end of Churchill it grew steadily worse; at its lowest ebb it was the most contemptible lot of rhymes ever tolerated without the precincts of Bedlam. The dreary inanities of Marvel, Tickell, Shenstone, Akenside and Young belong to the curiosities of literature, not to poetry. Pope turned the noble art into mere joiner's work, very neat and tasteful, but still joinery; and Johnson exhibited to the world how the thing was done by laboriously cutting up prose into five-foot lengths and squaring the ends, a process that needed only water-power or steam to run itself. No one in the whole English-speaking circuit from the Hebrides (by a stretch) to far Cathay, thought of poetry as an art. It was merely a neat and handy vehicle for one of three purposes:

Item, to express an attenuated sentiment about a lady's hand, looking-glass, glove or what-not foolery.

Item, to express to a waiting world some foolish person's foolish belief about creeds and policies.

Item, to express Mr. Dryden's personal contempt for Mr. Shadwell and vice versa.

In these unspeakable depths dwelt the glorious maid for one hundred and twenty-five years, heaven help all concerned.

Very likely the human mind went with her. From the restoration of the Stuarts for one hundred years the world progressed little. Sloth and sensuality gripped the fortunate; ignoble content laid its leaden mace on the toilers. Wars there were, but none that made for the benefit of mankind, one king warring against another for a bit of land or a wormy title or something equally worthless. Prose became (except for Swift) pointless twaddle; superstition had youthful science bound and gagged; the universities rumbled around the circles of classicism, lost to the world in fogs of their own making; educated people believed in witches and ghosts and that the touch of a fat dull king's forefinger was fatal to bacteria. Nobody discovered anything except new ways to make pork-pies. The throne ruled, the church ruled, the people slept; and for any man to get outside the smooth, main traveled path was lunacy.

In the end some one was certain to revolt. You might say in the end some one was certain to discover America, but we do not stop to think of that when we honor Christopher Columbus, plunging with three skiffs into the night of unknown seas.

In English literature the divine gift of revolt fell
upon a boy that killed himself when he was seventeen years and nine months old. He was the first
to break away from the juiceless formulas of pedantry,
he was the first to recognize the art possibilities of
medievalism, he was the first to see that the divine
art of poetry touches music with one hand and painting with the other, and has no mission but the mission
of her sister arts. He was the first person in one
hundred years to see that the music of speech might
be varied in verse to suit various emotions, that there
were limitless forms for limitless feelings, that the
iambic pentameter in rhymed couplets was not
necessarily sacred because it had been used by a little
man with a spiteful wit, and that poetry is not to be
made with a hammer. It was he that showed the different time-bars of English poetry and what they are
for. It was he, this boy, that started the movement
culminating in our age in the multitudinous varieties
of form and stanza and movement and beauty that
lay irresistible charm upon us in the poetry of
Tennyson and Swinburne. It is so, he was the
pioneer, this boy; there are fifty-seven measures in
the Rowley poems alone, and with the exception of
Herrick, that is more than you will find in any preceding English poet from Chaucer down.[1]   Here was

[1] But in the case of Herrick it should be remembered that the stanzaic variations
meant nothing but fantasy and a desire for novelty. In the case of Chatterton the
stanzaic form is invariably molded to the impression to be conveyed.

the spark that lighted the torch that fired the train. Coleridge came and saw how here the spray upsprang from the bird taking its flight, the cowslip trembled with the dew, the ripe apples bent the bough to the ground, and in line after line of his greatest singing you can see the result. One after another the poets that founded the modern school of art poetry came to this shrine; dumb to the world, the voice spoke clearly enough to them; they heard it reverently, Wordsworth, Shelley, Keats, this voice of the charity school boy that starved in London, and thousands of later singers repeat unconsciously what it taught these prophets.

What nature means to him is the measure of any artist. We know what it means to Swinburne and what it meant to Tennyson, Morris, Rossetti, Keats, Shelley, Wordsworth, as we see or hear the significance unfolded in those great word-pictures and word-symphonies. We do not stop to think that this intimate view of nature, this embracing sympathy and this purpose to paint her and sing her just as she is, trace, in their modern forms, straight back to Chatterton and no farther. The first definite suggestion that poetry is on one side a kind of painting was his; the first definite practise of poetry as painting to the imagination was his. The first practical recognition of the truth that to name an object does not necessarily call up a perfect vision of it, that it must be specified and illuminated and vitalized to the mind's eye, that was his also, and above all the firm underlying belief that the purpose of poetry is to transfer a feeling, not to preach sermons nor to elaborate metaphysics.

In these days we are so accustomed to such ideas we may not easily realize the time when they were not. But to see what was before Chatterton's time the poet's view of nature, take a few examples in which his predecessors deal with natural aspects. Abraham Cowley, for instance:

> In a deep vision's intellectual scene,
> Beneath a bower for sorrow made,
> Th' uncomfortable shade
> Of the black yew's unlucky green,
> Mixt with the mourning willow's careful gray,
> Where reverend Cham cuts out his famous way,
> The melancholy Cowley lay.

Or Andrew Marvell, "Thoughts in a Garden":

> No white nor red was ever seen
> So amorous as this lovely green.
> Fond lovers, cruel as their flame,
> Cut in these trees their mistress' name.
>
> .   .   .   .
>
> What wond'rous life is this I lead!
> Ripe apples drop about my head;
> The luscious clusters of the vine
> Upon my mouth do crush their wine;

> The nectarine, and curious peach,
> Into my hands themselves do reach;
> Stumbling on melons, as I pass,
> Ensnared with flowers, I fall on grass.

Or Denham, describing the Thames in "Cooper's Hill":

> My eye descending from the hill surveys
> Where Thames among the wanton valley strays:
> Thames, the most loved of all the Ocean's sons
> By his old sire, to his embraces runs:
> Hasting to pay his tribute to the sea,
> Like mortal life to meet eternity.
>
> .   .   .   .
>
> No unexpected inundations spoil
> The mower's hopes nor mock the ploughman's toil:
> But godlike his unwearied bounty flows;
> First loves to do, then loves the good he does.

Or Dryden lifting his voice to Mrs. Anne Killegrew:

> Thou youngest virgin-daughter of the skies,
> Made in the last promotion of the bless'd;
> Whose palms, new pluck'd from paradise,
> In spreading branches more sublimely rise,
> Rich with immortal green, above the rest:
> Whether, adopted to some neighb'ring star,
> Thou roll'st above us in thy wandering race.

Or Pope singing of Windsor Forest:

> Here hills and vales, the woodland and the plain,
> Here earth and water seem to strive again;
> Not chaos-like together crush'd and bruis'd,
> But as the world, harmoniously confus'd:

Where order in variety we see,
And where, though all things differ, all agree.
Here waving groves a chequer'd scene display,
And part admit, and part exclude the day.

Or Thomson, the admired artificer of the "Seasons" singing of Autumn:

But should a quicker breeze amid the boughs
Sob, o'er the sky the leafy deluge streams;
Till choked and matted with the dreary shower,
The forest walks, at every rising gale,
Roll wide the wither'd waste and whistle bleak.
Fled is the blasted verdure of the fields;
And, shrunk into their beds, the flowery race
Their sunny robes resign.

Or Thomson to the Nightingale:

O Nightingale, best poet of the grove,
    That plaintive strain can ne'er belong to thee,
Bless'd in the full possession of thy love:
    Oh, lend that strain, sweet Nightingale, to me!

In other words, nature was to all these and their fellows a sealed book. They saw the cover, of the contents they knew naught. All flowers looked alike to them; the field was but a field. To see how different it is to those that had really communed with her, we need but compare Thomson's "Nightingale" with Keats's, or Pope's daubed blur of "Windsor Forest" with any one of one hundred pictures in Rossetti — "The Day Dream," to pick one at random. And to see how the boy Chatterton was of the new school and not of the old, we should read together Thomson's feeble lines on "Autumn" with that immortal picture:

> When Autumn, bleak and sun-burnt, doth appear,
> With his gold hand gilding the falling leaf,
> Bringing up Winter to fulfil the year,
> Bearing upon his back the ripened sheaf.

The passing of the storm in the "Excelente Balade of Charitie" is the first attempt in English to utilize towards a designed effect both the sound resources and the picture resources of the language, and the song to Birtha in "Aella," "Oh Sing unto my Roundelay," is the first attempt after Milton's "L'Allegro" to make a word melody directly accordant with the sense. The pictures scattered through the Rowley poems, as of Spring, beginning "The budding floweret blushes at the light"; of morning, "The morn begins along the East to shine"; the vital images of particular scenes, the clean workmanship and the controlling view, which is always strictly that of the artist, always of one possessed of a certain definite feeling and striving to transfer that feeling to others, crown this boy as the first of the new school.

This excellent city of Bristol, that now gathers so

St. Mary Redcliffe, from the North.

(The monument to Chatterton is a little to the left of the center of the picture.)

intelligently and guards so jealously the memorials of her greatest son, was long accused of indifference to his fame. Perhaps unjustly; but seventy years ago there was a vicar of St. Mary Redcliffe that obstinately refused to permit a monument of Chatterton to stand in the churchyard, and thus he clouded the city's reputation. Yet I find in the City Library of Bristol an interesting pamphlet giving an account of an honor paid to Chatterton's memory that has hitherto escaped the notice of his biographers. The pamphlet bears this title:

The Ode, Songs, Choruses, &c.

For the Concert in

Commemoration of Chatterton, the Celebrated Bristol Poet,

As it was performed at the Assembly Room in Prince's

Street, Bristol, on Friday, the 3rd of December,

1784.

Written by Mr. Jenkins.

Dear is his memory to us, and long
Long, shall his attributes be known in song.
— Chatterton's Miscellanies.

London:

Printed and Sold by J. Bew, Paternoster Row

(Price One Shilling.)

The pamphlet begins with a short and not wholly correct account of Chatterton's life, in which for instance the date of his death is said to be August 22, but no one can think that it is unappreciative. On the programme performed on this interesting occasion was a "New Overture," a "Song by Miss Twist," a piece played by a quartette of violins and clarinets, a "Glee," sung by three voices, Messrs. Blanchard, Wordsworth, and Russel, with an oboe concerto; a "Song by Mr. Wordsworth" with a violin concerto, and a duet; after which came the reading of the ode in honor of Chatterton. This ode was an elaborate composition. It began with a chorus:

> Strike the Lyre, the Trumpet sound,
>   Wake to Joy each silent string,
> Let the vaulted Roof rebound,
>   While the immortal Bard we sing:
> While we proclaim our darling Son,
> Our pride, our Glory — Chatterton!

This was followed by two airs for solo female voices, a recitative and a final chorus as follows:

> Swell the loud Strain, to Rapture raise each Voice,
> Let drooping Genius and her Sons rejoice!
> And thou, our Avon, proudly roll along
> And to thy hallow'd namesake bear the Song,
> Tell the Vain River, that thy Stream hath lost
> Almost as sweet a Swan as hers could boast.

The monument was proposed about 1838, and there is still extant an indignant letter to the "Ad-

mirers of Chatterton," written in that year by one
E. M. Bath, in which the project is severely denounced
on the ground that Thomas Rowley was the real
poet and that in honoring Chatterton the town
would be honoring a mere transcriber of another
man's works. The letter has further interest from
the fact that its author is one of the very few men
that have found Horace Walpole's conduct towards
Chatterton to be admirable. It also defends Bristol
from the charge of indifference to the boy's memory,
arguing that there was nothing about him worth
remembering. But the money for the monument
was secured in spite of these cogent reasonings, and
the work was completed, when the project encountered
an unforeseen obstacle in the vicar. His ground of
opposition was that Chatterton had been an unbe-
liever, that he had told untruths, that he had taken
his own life in defiance of the law of the church in
such cases made and provided, and it was not for
the morals of the young that one so depraved should
be remembered. From this view no arguments
could move him; but he finally consented to a com-
promise. He agreed to allow the monument to be
erected provided it were inscribed with nine lines of his
selecting from Young's "Night Thoughts," consisting of a thundering condemnation of infidels. The
proponents of the monument felt the insult intended
upon the boy's memory, but rather than that he

should longer be unhonored they consented. The memorial was accordingly raised on the north side of the church, where had originally stood some miserable dwelling houses and where the ground was consequently unconsecrated and not liable to be harmed by a monument to a boy that had been driven to suicide. But it had not long been in place when the vestry determined to restore the North Porch. How the monument interfered with the restoration I cannot say, but on the ground of such interference the vicar ordered the stone removed, and for years it lay neglected in the crypt. At last the "obstinate heretic" of a vicar being removed or dying, a successor proved to be of good sense, and permitted the monument to be reinstated. It may do ease to those careful of such matters to know that it is still outside the lines of consecrated ground. It stands in the churchyard on the north and somewhat to the east of the North Porch. A pedestal and low shaft of a gray limestone are surmounted by a statue of a boy in the uniform of the Blue Coat school. Young's turgid verses have been erased and in their place appear the beautiful lines from Coleridge's "Monody," beginning "Sweet flower of hope!"

One side bears this:

A Posthumous Child, Born in this Parish, 20th November, 1752. Died in London, 24th August, 1770, aet. 18.

Admitted into Colston's School, 3rd August, 1760.

Dunelmus Bristolensis, 1768.

Rowlie MCCCCXXXXXXIX 1769.

Another side bears verses by the Rev. J. Eagles:

> A poor and friendless boy was he to whom
> Is raised this monument without a tomb.
> There seek his dust, there o'er his genius sigh,
> Where famished outcasts unrecorded lie.
> Here let his name, for here his genius rose
> To might of ancient days, in peace repose.
> The wondrous boy! to more than want consigned,
> To cold neglect, worse famine of the mind.
> All uncongenial the bright world within
> To that without of darkness and of sin.
>
> He lived a mystery — died — Here reader pause;
> Let God be judge and Mercy plead the cause.

And there on a tablet by itself is that simple and touching epitaph of his own designing:

"TO THE MEMORY OF

THOMAS CHATTERTON

Reader, judge not. If thou art a Christian, believe that he shall be judged by a supreme power; to that power alone is he now answerable."

We shall never know the face of this marvelous boy, for it may be taken for certain that there is no picture of him extant. The engraved portrait prefixed to the "Life" of Chatterton written by Dix is absolutely fraudulent. Strange how every phase of this story has been distorted by errant zeal or intentional deception so that from it every modern investigator comes with a new sense of the untrustworthiness of accepted statement! This picture that Dix printed is not only an instance in point but has a story well worth telling on its own account. A few years ago the literary world was astonished by the publication in the London *Atheneum* of the discovery of a genuine and undoubted portrait of Chatterton in the possession of the family of the late Sir Henry Taylor, author of "Philip van Artevelde." The publication was made in good faith and on such authority that the fact seemed indisputable. That the world had not before known what so many men had sought was easily accounted for by the fact that Sir Henry lived a very retired life at Kensington and few persons had opportunity to know of his treasure. The portrait was vouched for by an inscription on the back, and was accompanied by a statement that seemed extremely plausible. It had been painted for Chatterton's mother; after Mrs. Chatterton's death it had passed to her daughter, then become Mrs. Newton. Robert Southey, the laureate, had been very kind to Mrs. Newton. She had rewarded his kindness by giving him this portrait. At Southey's death it had been acquired by Wordsworth, whose sister had eventually presented it to Sir Henry Taylor. A discovery of this importance, involving so many famous names, naturally aroused keen interest. A controversy broke out that resembled in a small way the combats over Rowley. The truth was hard to arrive at. The story seemed as well authenticated as anything of the kind could be, and yet it was on the face of it most unlikely. The picture was of a boy seven, or at the most eight years old, and yet it was dated 1762. In 1762 Chatterton was ten, and it was agreed on all hands that he was unusually mature in his looks. The picture showed a boy in a red coat. In 1762 Chatterton was wearing the blue coat of the Colston uniform. The picture showed a boy with black or dark brown hair and with dark eyes. It was well established that Chatterton's hair was flaxen and his eyes were gray. In 1762 Mrs. Chatterton was struggling hard for daily bread; it was not possible that she could have afforded the luxury of a portrait. Moreover, there were the pilgrims to Bristol and the various investigators that had hunted so many years for such a picture and found no trace of it. And yet the statements of the inscription were as explicit as could be desired.

At last, after a patient investigation, aided by the willing cooperation of gentlemen in Bristol whose grandfathers or great-grandfathers had known the facts, the truth was disclosed. The picture was really the work of a Bristol artist named Morris, who painted it as a study of his own son. Years afterward it was engraved by a Bristol engraver as a specimen of his work and skill. In 1837, when Dix was in Bristol gathering information for his "Life," walking down a street one day with George Burge they came upon this engraving in the engraver's shop window. Burge suggested that the face might have resembled Chatterton. That is all we know positively, but the next we hear of the portrait it reappeared in Dix's book as a veritable picture of Chatterton. It is charitable to suppose that Dix was deceived in some way, but difficult to imagine the way. Dix's error, if it were only an error and not an intentional fraud, fixed a like blunder upon the original painting, but the details of the transmission through the hands of Southey and Wordsworth can only be guessed at. Mrs. Newton never gave the picture to Southey, but he may have had it in another way, and some fertile imagination like that of Dix may have supplied the rest of the story. Whatever was the origin of the fabrication it was strong enough to deceive Sir Henry Taylor. As an interesting side-light on what men do, not knowing what they do, it may be recalled that Dix printed a letter from Southey cordially endorsing the engraved portrait of the painter's son on the ground that it resembled Mrs. Newton. As he had never seen Chatterton this was as far as Southey could go. It appears that Dix was willing to go farther.

I offer this remarkable story as an illustration of the strange fatality that from the first has overhung this boy, and clouded with untruth everything connected with him, untruth that has injured both his artistic standing and his personal reputation. As an example of the first I cite the general assumption that he was inspired to his imitations by the example of Macpherson, and that he was, therefore, the imitator of an impostor, the second power of a fraud; whereas the truth is that the greater part of the Rowley poems was completed before Chatterton had seen or heard of Ossian. As a specimen of the second and still commoner injustice I remind you of the assertion that he was from his childhood of a sullen and perverse disposition, incorrigible and even depraved, whereas in truth he was most kindly, gentle, generous, and affectionate; inclined to melancholy thought, indeed, but never sullen, and really possessed of high ideals.

General recognition has come tardily to him because of the prejudice created by that absurd charge of "forgery," because of the other prejudice aroused by his democratic faith, and again because of the apparent difficulty of reading and judging his work, a difficulty due solely to his imitations of antique spelling and phraseology. These are but temporary and superficial barriers. No man in English literature is surer of his eventual fame. After all, prejudice is but a mortal growth and evanescent: the work it has overrun remains forever. Year by year the world views with more compassion the struggles of this sorely tried and lonely soul, with more tears the few little footsteps wandering in the dark, with more admiration the clarity of the genius that shone through all. Year by year, more of us, I think, perceive how just and true was the estimate of Dante Gabriel Rossetti, when he unhesitatingly placed Thomas Chatterton among the greatest poets and most amazing minds that have lighted the ways of men.

APPENDIX

I

HISTORIE OF PEYNCTERS YN ENGLANDE
Bie T. Rowlie

[This document accompanied Chatterton's second letter to Walpole.]

HAVEYNGE sayde yn oder places of peyncteynge and the ryse thereof, eke of somme peyncteres; nowe bee ytte toe be sayde of oders wordie of note. Afwolde was a skylled wyghte yn laieynge onne of coloures; hee lyved yn Merciæ, ynne the daies of Kynge Offa, ande depycted the countenaunce of Eadburga, his dawter, whyche depycture beeynge borne to Bryghtrycke he toke her to wyfe, as maie be seene at large in Alfridus.[1] Edilwald, Kynge of the Northumbers, understode peyncteynge, botte I cannot fynde anie piece of hys nemped.[2] Inne a mansion at Copenhamme I have seene a peyncteynge of moche antiquite, where is sitteynge Egbrychte in a royaul mannere, wythe kynges yn chaynes at hys fote, wythe meincte semblable [3] fygures whyche were symboles of hys lyfe; and I haveth noted the Saxons to be more notable ynne lore and peyncteynge thann the Normannes, nor ys the monies sythence the daies of Willyame

---

[1] This is a writer whose works I have never been happy enough to meet with.
[2] *Nemped* — mentioned.   [3] *Semblable* — metaphorical.

le Bastarde so fayrelie stroken as aforetyme.   I eke haveth
seene the armorie of East Sexe most fetyvelie [1] depycted,
ynn the medst of an auntyaunte wall.   Botte nowe we bee
upon peyncteynge, sommewhatte maie bee saide of the
poemes of these daies, whyche bee toe the mynde what
peyncteynge bee toe the eyne, the coloures of the fyrste
beeynge mo dureynge.   Ecca Byshoppe of Hereforde yn
D. LVII. was a goode poete, whome I thus Englyshe: —

Whan azure skie ys veylde yn robes of nyghte
    Whanne glemmrynge dewe droppes stounde [2] the faytours [3] eyne,
Whanne flying cloudes, betinged wyth roddie lyghte,
    Doth on the bryndlynge wolfe and wood bore shine,
Whanne even star, fayre herehaughte of nyghte,
Spreds the darke douskie sheene along the mees,[4]
    The wrethynge neders [5] sends a glumie [6] lyghte,
        And houlets wynge from levyn [7] blasted trees.
    Arise mie spryghte and seke the distant delle,
    And there to echoing tonges thie raptured joies ytele.

Gif thys manne han no hande for a peynter, he had a
head; a pycture appearethe ynne each lyne, and I wys so
fyne an even sighte mote be drawn as ynne above.   In
anoder of hys vearses he saithe: —

    Whanne sprynge came dauncynge onne a flourette bedde,
        Dighte ynne greene raimente of a chaungynge kynde;
    The leaves of hawthorne boddeynge on hys hedde,
        And wythe prymrosen coureynge to the wynde:

---

[1] *Fetyvelie* — elegantly, handsomely.   [2] *Stounde* — astonish.
[3] *Faytours* — travellers.   [4] *Mees* — mead.
[5] *Neders* — adders, used here perhaps as a glow-worm.
[6] *Glumie* — dull, gloomy.   [7] *Levyn* — blasted by lightning.

Thanne dydd the Shepster [1] hys longe albanne [2] spredde
   Uponne the greenie bancke and daunced rounde
Whilest the soest flowretes nodded onne his hedde,
   And hys fayre lambes besprenged [3] onne the grounde,
Anethe hys fote the brooklette ranne alonge,
Whyche strolleth rounde the vale to here his joyous songe.

Methynckethe these bee thoughtes notte oft to be metten wyth, and ne to bee excellede yn theyre kynde. Elmar, Byshoppe of Selesie, was fetyve yn workes of ghastlieness,[4] for the whyche take yee thys speeche: —

Nowe maie alle helle open to glope thee downe,
   Whylst azure merke [5] immenged [6] wythe the daie,
Shewe lyghte on darkned peynes to be moe roune,[7]
   O mayest thou die lyvinge deathes for aie:
Maie floodes of Solfirre bear thie sprighte anoune [8]
   Synkeynge to depths of woe, maie levynne brondes [9]
Tremble upon thie peyne devoted crowne,
   And senge thie alle yn vayne emploreynge hondes;
Maie all the woes that Godis wrathe can sende
Upon thie heade alyghte, and there theyre furie spende.

Gorweth of Wales be sayde to be a wryter goode, botte I understande notte that tonge. Thus moche for poetes, whose poesies do beere resemblance to pyctures in mie unwordie opynion. Asserius was wryter of hystories; he ys buryed at Seyncte Keynas College ynne Keynshamm

[1] *Shepster* — shepherd.
[2] *Albanne* — a large loose white robe.
[3] *Besprenged* — scattered.
[4] *Ghastlieness* — terror.
[5] *Merke* — darkness.
[6] *Immenged* — mingled.
[7] *Roune* — terrific.
[8] *Anoune* — ever and anon.
[9] *Levynne brondes* — thunderbolts.

wythe Turgotte, anoder wryter of hystories, Inne the walle
of this college ys a tombe of Seyncte Keyna [1] whych was
ydoulven anie, and placed ynne the walle, albeit done yn
the daies of Cerdyke, as appeared bie a crosse of leade
upon the kyste;[2] ytte bee moe notablie performed than
meynte [3] of ymageries [4] of these daies. Inne the chyrche
wyndowe ys a geason [5] peyncteynge of Seyncte Keyna
syttynge yn a trefoliated chayre, ynne a long alban braced
wythe golden gyrdles from the wayste upwarde to the
breaste, over the whyche ys a small azure coape;[6] benethe
ys depycted Galfridus, MLV. whyche maie bee that Geof-
froie who ybuylded the geason gate [7] to Seyncte Augustynes
chapele once leadynge. Harrie Piercie of Northomber-
lande was a quaynte [8] peyncter; he lyvede yn M. C. and
depycted severalle of the wyndowes ynne Thonge Abbye,
the greate windowe atte Battaile Abbeie; he depycted the
face verie welle wythalle, botte was lackeynge yn the most-
to-bee-loked-to-accounte, proportione. John a Roane
payncted the shape of a hayre: he carved the castle for the
sheelde of Gilberte Clare of thek [9] feytyve performaunce.
Elwarde ycorne [10] the castle for the seal of Kynge Harolde
of most geason worke; nor has anie seale sythence bynne so
rare, excepte the seale of Kinge Henrie the fyfthe, corven
by Josephe Whetgyfte. Thomas a Baker from corveynge
crosse loafes, tooke to corveying of ymageryes, whych he

---

[1] This I believe is there now.   [2] *Kyste* — coffin.

[3] *Meynte* — many.   [4] *Ymageries* — statues, etc.

[5] *Geason* — curious.   [6] *Coape* — cloak or mantle.

[7] This gate is now standing in this city, though the chapel is not to be seen.

[8] *Quaynte* — curious.   [9] *Thek* — very.

[10] *Ycorne* — a contraction of ycorven, carved.

dyd most fetyvelie; he lyved ynne the cittie of Bathe, beeynge
the fyrste yn Englande, thatte used hayre ynne the bowe
of the fyddle,[1] beeynge before used wythe peetched hempe
or flax. Thys carveller dyd decase yn MLXXI. Thus
moche for carvellers and peyncters.

[Comment by Chatterton.]

John was inducted abbot in the year 1146, and sat in the
dies 29 years. As you approve of the small specimen of
his poetry, I have sent you a larger, which though admirable is still (in my opinion) inferior to Rowley [2] whose
works when I have leisure I will fairly copy and send you.

[1] Nothing is so much wanted as a History of the Antiquity of the Violin, nor is
any antiquary more able to do it than yourself. Such a piece would redound to
the honour of England, as Rowley proves the use of the bow to be knowne to the
Saxons, and even introduced by them.

[2] None of Rowley's pieces were ever made public, being, till the year 1631, shut
up in the iron chest in Redcliffe Church.

II

WILLIAM CANYNGE

[The following extracts are from Mr. George Pryce's "Memorials of the Canynges' Family and their Times," Bristol, 1854; an interesting book to which I am under very great obligations for information, much of it now inaccessible elsewhere.]

TOWARDS the close of the year in which William Canynges for the fourth time occupied the chair of Bristol's Chief Magistrate, the old town was visited by King Edward IV, who was then on a tour through the Western Counties. In recording this visit, quaint old John Stow informs his readers that "in the harvest season, King Edward rode to Canterbury and to Sandwich, and so along by the sea coast to Hampton, and from thence into the Marches of Wales, and to Bristow, where he was most royally received"; and the following very curious account of the pageant which welcomed him is supplied by the learned editor of Warkworth's *Chronicle*, in his notes appended to that volume.[1] It commences with

"The receyvyng of Kyng Edward iiij[th] at Brystowe.

"First, at the comying inne atte temple gate, there stode Wylliam Conquerour, with iij. lordis, and these were his wordis: —

[1] This example from a genuine old chronicle should be compared with Chatterton's account of the opening of the old bridge and the specimens of his work in the antique style.

'Wellcome Edwarde! oure son of high degre;
Many yeeris hast thou lakkyd owte of this londe —
I am thy forefader, Wylliam of Normandye,
To see thy welefare here through Goddys sond.'

"Over the same gate stondyng a greet Gyant delyveryng the keyes.

"The Receyvyng atte Temple Crosse next following; —

"There was Seynt George on horsbakke, uppon a tent, fyghtyng with a dragon; and the Kyng and the Quene on hygh in a castell, and his doughter benethe with a lambe; and atte the sleying of the dragon ther was a great melody of aungellys."

.   .   .   .

The welcome given to the king by William Canynges, and the feasting of the monarch in his house, has been already sufficiently noticed; but the particulars of the visit, so far as it regards the wealthy merchant's commercial affairs, (and upon the prosperous state of which the sovereign calculated he should exact, in conjunction with aids from other opulent traders in the old town, the forced loan before referred to,) require more than a merely passing remark.

It appears that on his arrival, Edward commenced taking stock of the port; that is, the number of vessels belonging to each individual and their value was carefully ascertained; and then a certain amount, not mentioned, was assessed upon them to be paid to the King. Although the names and tonnage of the vessels possessed by other merchants at this time in Bristol are not recorded, those belonging to William Canynges have been noted by William of Wyrcestre, and described as follows: — The Mary Canynges, 400 tons burthen; the Mary Radclyf, 500 tons;

Mary and John, 900 tons; the Galyot, 50 tons; the Cateryn, 140 tons; the Marybat, 220 tons; the Margyt de Tynly, 200 tons; the lytylle Nicholas, 140 tons; the Kateryn de Boston, 220 tons; the . . . . . ship, in Iselond, (not Ireland, as Mr. Barrett calls it,) 160 tons; in the whole, 2853 tons of shipping, manned by 800 mariners.

In this year also Canynges again evidenced his love of Mother Church, as appears by the following which occurs among the "City Benefactions," recorded by Barrett: —

"1466.   William Canynges gave by deed for
                divine offices in Redcliffe Church 340 0 0
                And in plate to the said Church: 160 0 0
                                                                                              ————
Vested in the vicar and proctors of Redcliffe: . . . . . . £500 0 0"

To this donation I shall have occasion to refer at greater length when treating of the structure named in the bequest.

The Mayor's Calendar, by Robert Ricaut, preserved in the archives of the Corporation, under date of 1467, says: "This yere the said William Canynges Maire shulde have be (been) maired (married) by the Kyng our Souverain Lord comandement as it was saide Wherefore the said Canynges gave up the Worlde and in all haste toke ordirs upon hym of the gode Bisshop of Worcestre called Carpynter, and was made Preest and sange his furst Masse at our Lady of Redclif the yere folowying R Jakys beeng Maire at Whitsontide and after that he was Dean of Westbury certein years & dececed & was buried Worshipfully at Redeclif by his Wife in the south ende of the Medyll yle of the saide Churche."

III

CANYNGE AND ROWLEY

[This specimen of Rowley's Prose is taken from "Chatterton's Miscellanies," London, 1778. It is called "Some farther Account of this Extraordinary Person [Canynge] written by Rowley the Priest."]

I WAS fadre confessor to masteres Roberte and mastre William Cannings. Mastre Robert was a man after his fadre's own harte, greedie of gaynes and sparynge of alms deedes; but master William was mickle courteous, and gave me many marks in my needs. At the age of 22 years deaces'd master Roberte, and by master William's desyre bequeathed me one hundred marks; I went to thank master William for his mickle courtesie, and to make tender of myselfe to him. — Fadre quode he, I have a crotchett in my brayne, that will need your aide. Master William, said I, if you command me I will go to Roome for you; not so farr distant, said he: I ken you for a mickle learnd priest; if you will leave the parysh of our ladie, and travel for mee, it shall be mickle to your profits.

I gave my hands, and he told mee I must goe to all the abbies and pryorys, and gather together auncient drawyings, if of anie account, at any price. Consented I to the same, and pursuant sett out the Mundaie following for the minister of our Ladie and Saint Goodwyne, where a drawing of a steeple, contryvd for the belles when runge to swaie out of the syde into the ayre, had I thence; it was done by Syr Symon de Mambrie, who, in the troublesomme rayne of kyng Stephen, devoted himselfe, and was shorne.

Hawkes showd me a manuscript in Saxonne, but I was onley to bargayne for drawyings. — The next drawyings I metten with was a church to be reard, so as in form of a cross, the end standing in the ground; a long manuscript was annexd. Master Canning thought no workman culd be found handie enough to do it. — The tale of the drawers deserveth relation. — Thomas de Blunderville, a preeste, although the preeste had no allows, lovd a fair mayden, and on her begatt a sonn. Thomas educated his sonn; at sixteen years he went into the warrs, and neer did return for five years. — His mother was married to a knight, and bare a daughter, then sixteen, who was seen and lovd by Thomas, sonn of Thomas, and married to him, unknown to her mother, by Ralph de Mesching, of the minister, who invited, as custom was, two of his brothers, Thomas de Blunderville and John Heschamme. Thomas nevertheless had not seen his sonn for five years, yet kennd him instauntly; and learning the name of the bryde, took him asydde and disclosd to him that he was his sonn, and was weded to his own sistre. Yoynge Thomas toke on so that he was shorne.

He drew manie fine drawyings on glass.

The abott of the minster of Peterburrow sold it me; he might have bargaynd 20 marks better, but master William would not part with it. The prior of Coventree did sell me a picture of great account, made by Badilian Y'allyanne, who did live in the reign of Kynge Henrie the First, a mann of fickle temper, havyng been tendred syx pounds of silver for it, to which he said naie, and afterwards did give it to the then abott of Coventriee. In brief, I gathered together manie marks value of fine drawyings, all the works of mickle cunning. — Master William culld the most choise parts, but hearing of a drawying in Durham church hee did send me.

Fadree, you have done mickle well, all the chatills are more worth then you gave; take this for your paynes: so saying, he did put into my hands a purse of two hundreds good pounds, and did say that I should note be in need; I did thank him most heartily. — The choice drawying, when his fadre did dye, was begunn to be put up, and somme houses neer the old church erased; it was drawn by Aflema, preeste of St. Cutchburts, and offerd as a drawyng for Westminster, but cast asyde, being the tender did not speak French. — I had now mickle of ryches, and lyvd in a house on the hyll, often repayrings to mastere William, who was now lord of the house. I sent him my verses touching his church, for which he did send me mickle good things. — In the year kyng Edward came to Bristow, master Cannings send for me to avoid a marrige which the kyng was bent upon between him and a ladie he neer had seen, of the familee of the Winddevilles; the danger were nigh, unless avoided by one remidee, an holie one, which was, to be ordained a sonn of holy church, beyng franke from the power of kynges in that cause, and cannot be wedded. — Mr. Cannings instauntly sent me to Carpenter, his good friend, bishop of Worcester, and the Fryday following was prepaird and ordaynd the next day, the daie of St. Mathew, and on Sunday sung his first mass in the church of our Ladie, to the astonishing of kyng Edward, who was so furiously madd and ravyngs withall, that master Cannings was wyling to give him 3000 markes, which made him peace again, and he was admyted to the presence of the kyng, staid in Bristow, partook of all his pleasures and pastimes till he departed the next year.

I gave master Cannings my Bristow tragedy, for which he gave me in hands twentie pounds, and did praise it more then I did think my self did deserve, for I can say in troth I was never proud of my verses since I did read master Chaucer; and now haveing nought to do, and not wyling to be ydle, I went to the minster of our Ladie and Saint Goodwin, and then did purchase the Saxon manuscripts, and sett my selfe diligentley to translate and worde it in English metre, which in one year I performd and styled it the Battle of Hastyngs; master William did bargyin for one manuscript, and John Pelham, an esquire, of Ashley, for another. — Master William did praise it muckle greatly, but advisd me to tender it to no man, beying the menn whose name were therein mentiond would be offended. He gave me 20 markes, and I did goe to Ashley, to master Pelham, to be payd of him for the other one I left with him.

But his ladie being of the family of the Fiscamps, of whom some things are said, he told me he had burnt it, and would have me burnt too if I did not avaunt. Dureing this dinn his wife did come out, and made a dinn to speake by a figure, would have over sounded the bells of our Ladie of the Cliffe; I was fain content to gett away in a safe skin.

I wrote my Justice of Peace, which master Cannings advisd me secrett to keep, which I did; and now being grown auncient I was seizd with great pains, which did cost me mickle of marks to be cured off. — Master William offered me a cannon's place in Westbury-College, which gladly had I accepted but my pains made me to stay at home. After this mischance I livd in a house by the Tower, which has not been repaird since Robert Consull of Gloucester repayrd the castle and wall; here I livd warm, but in my house on the hyll the ayer was mickle keen; some marks it cost me to put in repair my new house; and brynging my chattles from the ould; it was a fine house, and I much marville it was untenanted. A person greedy of gains was the then possessour, and of him I did buy it at a very small rate, having lookd on the ground works and mayne supports, and fynding them staunch, and repayrs no need wanting, I did buy of the owner, Geoffrey Coombe, on a repayring lease for 99 years, he thinkying it would fall down everie day; but with a few marks expence did put it up a manner neat, and therein I lyvd.

IV

THE ROWLEY CONTROVERSY

[Specimen Pages from "Bryant's Observations." He is treating of the "Battle of Hastings," No. 1.]

I CANNOT quit this subject without mentioning a passage in the poet, which may perhaps further illustrate, what I have been saying. In the beginning of the Battle of Hastings, there is a noble apostrophe made to the sea: concerning whose influence the poet speaks with regret: as it was not exerted to the destruction of the Normans.

> O sea, our teeming donore, han thy floud
>> Han anie fructuous entendement,
> Thou wouldst have rose and sank wyth tydes of bloude,
>> Before Duke William's Knyghts han hither went:
> Whose cowart arrows menie erles (have) sleyne,
>> And brued the feeld wyth bloude as season rayne.

p. 210.

I mention this, because I think, that we may perceive here a tacit reference to an event; which at first sight is not obvious. The author in his address to the sea seems to say, had thy flood been calculated for any good, it would have arisen, before the Norman navy had reached our shores: and preserved us from that fatal invasion. When therefore he says, had thy flood had any good intention, it is natural to ask, *when:* and *upon what occasion.* For by the tenour of the words he seems to refer to a time; and allude to some particular crisis. And when he adds, after this intimation, that it would then have risen before the landing of the Normans, he seems to indicate, that it had risen, but at a less favourable season. It appears, therefore, to me, that there is in this passage to be observed one of those occult allusions, of which I made mention before. There is certainly a retrospect to an event, well known in the age of the writer: and that event was an overflowing of the sea. Now it is remarkable, that at the time, when I suppose the first sketch of this poem to have been produced, there were great inundations upon the southern coasts of England, which are taken notice of by several of our historians. They happened in the latter part of the reign of William Rufus, and in the early part of that of his successor. That in the time of Rufus is mentioned, as very extraordinary in its effects; and consequently very alarming. The author of the Saxon Chronicle speaks of its being attended with the greatest damages ever known. The like is recorded by Simeon of Durham. Mare littus egreditur; et villas et homines quam plures, etc., demersit. Florence of Worcester writes to the same purpose. Great part of Zealand is said at this time to have suffered: and the Goodwin sands are supposed to have been formed by this inundation, which before did not appear.

Mr. Tyrwhitt thinks, that, instead of O Sea, our teeming Donore, the true reading was, O, sea-o'er-teeming Dover. This is a very ingenious alteration, and I think highly probable. But instead of forming a decompound, I should rather separate the second term, and read, O Sea, o'er-teeming Dover: for the address must be to the sea, and not to the place: as the poet in the third verse speaks of its rising. Now to teem signifies to abound and to be pro-lifick: also to pour and fill. Hence we find in Ainsworth, teemful, brimful. The same also occurs in Ray's North Country words: To teem, to pour out, or lade. Also teem-ful, brimful, having as much as can be teemed in; *i.e.* poured in. p. 60, 61. Accordingly, o'er-teeming must signify overflowing, pouring over. When therefore the poet addresses himself to this o'er-teeming sea, he seems to allude to that general inundation, by which Dover, and many other places upon the southern coast of this island, were overwhelmed. Stow mentions that this flood did great mischief to many towns and villages upon the sides of the Thames: and it is said to have prevailed in the North, as high up as Scotland. But its chief fury seems to have been in the narrow seas of the channel; and upon those very coasts upon which a few years before the Normans had landed. It was natural for a writer of the times to allude to an event so recent; and to make a reference so obvious. And I do not know any person, to whom this address can with propriety be ascribed, but to Turgot. He was probably writing at the very time of this calamity: and nothing could be more natural than for him at such a season to make this apostrophe: which is very much illus-trated by the history of those times.

O Sea, o'er-teeming Dover, had thy flood had any good purpose to our country, it would have risen be-fore Duke William with his nobles had arrived upon our coasts: and have overwhelmed his army. This in great measure authenticates, what is said by Rowley, that this poem was a version from a Saxon manuscript: and it justifies his invocation of Turgot, to whom he was beholden for it.

INDEX

CPSIA information can be obtained
at www.ICGtesting.com
Printed in the USA
BVHW030218230621
610280BV00004B/23